PETER HAMM

Memoir

Happy Me!

Eagle House

First published in Great Britain under the title
Memoir: Happy Me! in 2005
by Eagle House

First Edition

Copyright © Peter Hammond 2005

The right of Peter Hammond to be identified as the author of this work has been asserted by him in accordance with the Copyright, Designs and Patents Act 1988.

All rights reserved. No part of this publication may be reproduced, stored in a retrieval system, or transmitted, in any form or by any means (electronic, mechanical, photocopying, recording or otherwise), without the prior written permission of the publisher, nor be otherwise circulated in any form of binding or cover other than that in which it is published and without a similar condition being imposed on the subsequent purchaser.

British Library Cataloguing in Publication Data
A record for this book is available from the British Library

ISBN: 0 9552138 0 0
ISBN: 978 0 9552138 0 9

Eagle House
P.O. Box 47130
London
W6 7WU
tel. 020 7602 9405

Set in Palatino

Printed and bound in England.

Acknowledgements

With grateful thanks to all my dear friends in my church community who have made this possible.

Contents

Chapters

1. Beginnings — 7
2. Home — 21
3. School, Evacuation & Teacher Training — 33
4. The Coalmines: 1944–47 — 43
5. Teaching — 51
6. The Christian Ministry: 1973–2000 — 61
7. Holidays and My Absorbing Interests — 67
8. The Blessed Present — 83
9. Summing up and Onward — 89

Chapter 1

Beginnings

My birth at home was long and strenuous for my mother, and the doctor. Afterwards he flung open the window, presumably from heat and exhaustion, and said to my parents "No more, no more". I believe he feared for my mother's life in any future pregnancy. My mother had a curvature of the bottom of the spine, which perhaps had aggravated the situation. So my birth may have been, as Wellington put it, "a damn close run thing". I was, as it was called then, "a breeches baby", born feet first. The morning afterwards my sister particularly remembered the blue veins in my eyelids, perhaps a sign of frailty. I remember singularly little of my earliest years.

My first concrete memory is that of an occasion when I was alone with my maternal grandmother and another lady of similar age. I had soiled myself and was screaming for help. My grandmother offered help which I violently refused, until my mother eventually returned and came to my aid. My grandmother was then 73 and this is the only occasion I remember seeing her. She wore a black dress down to her feet and a light gold necklace. I have a photograph of her that I cherish, showing a face of beautiful care and kindness. She died that same year of heart failure.

My mother loved her dearly, more than could be said of her relationship with her father. He had tried to over discipline my mother's fiery nature, even resorting to the slipper. She was not his favourite daughter. She probably had limited scholastic success (like her son), but learned shorthand and typing so efficiently that she became the first female trained thus, to work in the City of London. She cut off her fine red hair to suit the style of the time, to the horror of my grandfather, who said she looked like a "fallen woman"! Apparently my mother confided to her mother of having to deal with so much recalcitrance on my part. My mother replied to her suggesting that a child needed to grow up having determination and spirit.

When my grandmother was gravely ill she asked my mother if she was going to die. My mother, just about the most honest person I have ever met, said, "Well the doctor says you are very ill." My grandmother, a devout Christian, said, "Ah well, I shall see May and Will." May was a baby that had died in infancy and Will was her only son, who had been killed in the First World War, serving as a stretcher-bearer.

Our family was augmented by Rose, who had come to us as a live-in maid when my brother was born 3 years previously. She had her own room and was eventually paid a full man's wage, then about £3 per week. She rapidly became a member of the family and a friend to my mother. She stayed with us until I was about 14, putting up patiently with a wilful, aggressive, and rebellious child, who was yet sensitive. God bless her. I'm sure that, if our paths were to cross again, there would be many colourful stories she could tell about this "rebellious" child. My own memory of life from the age of five up to 14 remains jumbled.

At the age of five I started school at the local council school. My sister and brother had gone to Miss Rossiter's, a private school, but I guess cash must have been too short to send me there. On my first journey to school my eyes were watering, and my mother and Rose said I was crying. I replied, roughly, that it was the wind and the cold and I still think it was, after 75 years. On the first day I was kept in for fighting. My opponent was a Scottish lad called Douglas Roy. I am afraid this fighting habit continued, although perhaps ceasing, before I went to secondary school at the age of 11. I invariably came off worst. So disturbing was this to the staff, that the infants school headmistress threatened to cane me if I continued to lead a gang, a dreadful threat. Most of my opponents were from what was then considered a lower milieu. They were extremely tough, too. One memorable combat involved an amiable lad called Tappenden. He hit my jaw so shrewdly, that I collapsed. I was taken home in a pram by my class teacher, Mrs Payne, a lady of ample size with a limited dress sense. When my mother opened the door, she thought that a washerwoman had brought the washing to the wrong house. We did our own. It ensued that I had concussion. I can still vaguely remember the headaches. Poor Tappenden was caned by the headmaster, perhaps as a sop to my parents. The headmaster was a fearsome man, one of the few people I have really feared. One of his dark brown eyes was out of alignment and he later became blind. He was very dark and always wore a dark brown suit. Sadly his wife later left him. When I requested pre-college experience in teaching at his school, he was happy to allow this and I think gave me a good report. His deputy, Mr P, had served with him during the First World War and looked after him carefully. Mr P was large and friendly, and always wore a fawn Harris tweed suit. He was not to be trifled with however. He always taught the top class, boys up to the age of 14.

Another vivid memory was the day it was judged that I should have my tonsils and adenoids removed. I was still around five at the time. For the first time in my life, I had to be away from home at night and in a cottage hospital. After the lights went out I urgently wanted to use the toilet but could not find one. Being desperate, I asked an adult patient but had no help and there did not seem to be a nurse anywhere. I eventually went back to my bed and slept. In the morning I was woken by the formidable, though kindly matron. I had wet the bed. She took me up in her arms and comforted me. Bless her! I was then prepared for surgery. I remember the anaesthetist's mask for administering what I presume was chloroform. It was shaped like an inverted sieve. Then I was out like a light.

When I woke up I had a sore throat and the luxury of a car ride home. Once there I was put to bed and demanded sardine sandwiches with brown bread, still a favourite now. The other medical experience I remember, apart from the concussion, was when I had a very severe stomach upset and the doctor was called for. He said I had "strawberryitis". I had eaten some strawberries the previous day, though not an undue amount. He recommended a draught of orange juice, castor oil and brandy. This caused a problem, since as a committed Methodist family we did not drink alcohol. Eventually a small dusty bottle of brandy was discovered in a little cupboard, called "the medicine chest".

Another unpleasant experience concerns the school toilets at our council school. The urinals were in two sections with a wall between them that was just above my height. I was using the facility on one side with two older boys on the other. They were evidently competing to see who could project urine over the wall. One of them *did* and it splashed on me. I still remember the smell on my white fabric braces when it dried. I never told a teacher about this incident. One never "split" in those days. Readers will appreciate that my school environment was alien to a child from, what I suppose would be called today, a "lower middle class" home. Then I remember my first visit to the dentist.

On that day (there were no classy surgeries then), my father took me to buy a few small fireworks. He never wasted money because every penny counted in our family economy. Somehow I marvelled at a new penny dated 1930. I was mesmerised, for that was the year in which we were. I cannot understand why. Maybe it was an awesome sense of the passage of time lying entirely out of human control, an entity in itself.

Our modest garden had, at its end, a high wall, possibly as high as the top of the first storey of a house. It was not solid but consisted of two concrete skins with a timber framework in between. A rowan tree stood at the corner of our garden, which I learned to climb to survey the landscape. I used to ask Rose for a slice of toast left over from breakfast, to which I added plenty of butter and syrup. Then I would disappear to my haven (the top of the garden wall), where I would eat with joy. It was bliss!

I later developed an interest in poison and once made a potion of rowan berries, which I wrongly imagined to be poisonous. For one of my birthdays I was given a chemistry set. It naturally did not contain anything harmful, but included a booklet which described the chemical use of spirits of salts – hydrochloric acid. Secretly and greatly daring, I went to our local chemist, who having explained to me the dangers of such a corrosive acid, sold a bottle of it to me. The acid looked menacing in its strange, ribbed and dark green bottle. Soon after leaving the shop (perhaps the day might have been cold and I was wearing knitted gloves), the bottle slipped out of my hand and smashed on the pavement. I was dismayed and frightened. Thankfully, no one was in sight, so I hurried home.

I regularly played war games in various modes. We had a tool shed in the garden that my paternal grandfather had made. This shed became my playground where I regularly played, pretending that a timber, which I poked out of the window, was a naval gun. This went on until I was an evacuee at the age of 14. In fact, the last thing I did on the morning I left home was to make paper aeroplanes that held a few marbles, and drop them on toy soldiers from above.

It must be remembered that, this objectionable child craved affection. I came home at lunch-time from secondary school, school lunches being almost unheard of, and frequently asked to have a cuddle on Rose's lap. "Just five minutes" was the phrase. I was 11.

I was, as previously stated, a cheeky and aggressive child who always seemed to irritate older relatives, ~~who were~~ *was* easily hurt, yet did not seem to understand how provocative I was. My father loved gardening, but had little time for it. He was quietly distressed when I played garden cricket and was frequently knocking the heads off the few blooms he had managed to produce. (Garden cricket is to throw a ball against the wall and try to hit it with a bat on the rebound.) I was a thoughtless brat who persisted in the damage.

At my council school there was a scholarship offered each year to board at Christ's Hospital and another for a day place at Chigwell, a local public school. This was the school to which three of our Leng cousins attended as boarders. The cleverest boy in our class, one Buxton, was offered the Chigwell place but opted to go to Christ's

Hospital. I was then, to my terror, offered Chigwell, where the syllabus included Latin and Greek. I knew I had an inferior memory that could not retain the meaning of foreign words, let alone unknown conjugations and declensions. Mr Fellows, a form master at Chigwell, came to our home after my bedtime and I could hear him almost pleading with my parents. Though charming, I could sense that he was a rigid disciplinarian who might confuse my inability with laziness. I feared the future. My word! How I pleaded with my parents. I am so grateful that they allowed me to go to the local grammar school with my brother. Perhaps they understood me more than I realised.

I ought to mention at this point my relationship with my brother. He was three years older than I and I terrorised him. He had a totally different temperament to mine. I understand that he lacked confidence as a young child, unlike his brash sibling! He grew up meticulously neat and careful, conscientious and thorough in schoolwork as in everything else. He hated, for a lifetime, his work at an insurance office in London, where I am sure his quality of work was much appreciated. He married in his later 20s. He was a natural gentleman, completely unassertive and always seemed to defer to me. I was always hitting him, unprovoked, intending to rule his roost. A cousin once said that her picture of us was of me pursuing him home from Sunday School with a view to hitting him. He continued to love me, goodness knows why. He had the endearing habit in his teens of stopping up late and cooking very well done toast and cheese. A delightful odour used to waft up the stairs! He volunteered for war service in the RAF ground staff, where I am sure he made an excellent wireless operator. I still remember his RAF number – 1522671!

My sister, Cherry, was somewhat remote from me, regarding me accurately as a grubby little nuisance. She was very gifted and clearly one of the bright lights of her girls' grammar school. She was a tiny thing, so much so, that her formidable Scottish headmistress ordered her to have a glass of hot milk at school every day. *Ugh!* She yearned to go to Oxford in 1938 but we just could not afford it. She went instead to Westfield College, London, which by a happy chance, was evacuated to Oxford. There, a complete stranger saw her on a bus and thought to himself "I'm going to marry that girl", which he did. Her husband, Peter, was a quality student at one of the Oxford Colleges, reading Classics, I believe.

In the First World War he registered as a non-religious conscientious objector and worked throughout in the gruesome work of heavy rescue, presumably in London, while Cherry worked in housing. Cherry had much tragedy in her life. She lost their first child, aged two, from some strange throat condition. Peter died at the age of 37. He suffered a heart attack while playing squash. Of her two other children, Richard, the elder, aged 16, also died of a heart attack while out jogging. It was then discovered that he had died of a rare genetic blood condition which furred up the arteries to those of an elderly man. A new drug was later developed to treat this condition and Neil, Cherry and Peter's remaining son and his family have to be tested and treated appropriately. All are in good health.

Cherry was a person of few words. She never confided in me until the last year or two of her life. In her later years she lectured in English but was also considerably occupied with counselling students. She must have profoundly improved the lives and attitudes of hundreds of young people. She was, I believe, the most caring person I have ever known, apart from my father, and a far, far better person than I could ever hope to be. She used to go and stay with one of her college friends, the wife of a clergyman who ran a Christian community. This clergyman once told Cherry that he could not understand her kindness, she not being an avowed Christian. (She had abandoned Christianity and Methodism in her late teens.) She must have inherited from my father a deep Christian love. At her funeral service, which I was privileged to take, the large crematorium was filled with nearly 200 people.

Although I never went against my father's express wishes when he was present, my life was a continual lively contest with my mother. Once I pinched a lump of sugar from the bowl in the sideboard. I had a terrible wigging. I seem to have inherited this slightly obsessive honesty; I think our temperaments must have had a lot in common. She was never in very good health, having had a mastectomy in her early 40s, but always quietly supported by Rose.

I have not mentioned my stammer. This apparently started when I was about 3, and was a considerable cause of distress and misunderstanding until it diminished a good deal in teaching and in the ministry. It is worse in private conversation, more noticeable with family and friends, than in public speaking. I shall never forget a particular incident.

Our lives were built within our local Methodist church, part of our Methodist circuit or grouping of a number of Methodist churches. Each year there was a competition between the churches in our circuit, called the Eisteddfod, after the Welsh Eisteddfod. I was persuaded to enter for a song and a recitation in my age group. It was thought I had a good clear singing voice. But when I got up on the stage I was paralysed. It was dreadful, however understanding people were. I also received encouragement and soon regained confidence in my own ability. With renewed strength, I participated in the following activities.

I attended both morning and afternoon Sunday School, apart from the two adult services. At about 13 or 14 I was sometimes persuaded to lead the morning Sunday School worship. In the afternoon we had the usual graded classes. There, I was my usual attention-seeking self and made the sessions "a hell" for my earnest teacher. He presented me with a home-made but very effective and dangerous catapult. It made no difference. Eventually the Sunday School superintendent called me in for a chat. He was a lovely, gentle man, who was killed a few years afterwards in his home by a German landmine. Something, which I did not recognise, then clicked and changed me. I was promoted immediately to the senior fellowship, a young adults group, and began to listen with interest. I now recognise, of course, the source of my change in character.

At around the same age I was persuaded to join the local Scout troop. No pressure was applied by my parents, although they must have breathed a sigh of relief to see my cussedness under an extra discipline. The scoutmaster lived next door and was an interesting character. His name was Aubrey Cornwall, known to all the scouts as "Strawberry" Cornwall, on account of his nose being unduly large and red, and pitted like a strawberry. His wife, he being about 50, was very much younger than him and a rather timid woman, probably then in her 20s. She had a delightful Cornish accent. When I went into their home it seemed very different from ours. I was made to wait in a large tiled hall, which always seemed very quiet, apart from the loud, slow tick from a clock in the hall. A model with a complete suit of armour was the most striking feature in the hall. It was very small and must have been used as a model for armourers. Aubrey Cornwall had a clipped moustache and a clipped voice, together with an authoritative manner and, for his everyday work, was a proper and impeccable city gentleman with a bowler hat and a tightly rolled umbrella. An old bowler hat of his was once discovered at a scout jumble sale, price one penny. I bought it, somewhat to Aubrey's contempt. I passed the hat on to my brother who wore it to work in London. I suppose he was 16 or 17 then. Mr Cornwall took me for several drives in his splendid Invicta car before I joined the Scouts, perhaps as a form of bribery.

I did not have a proper scout uniform, due to the cost, but I inherited one from my cousin R, who had no further use for it. It was somewhat antiquated in design. We went to a weekend camp at Gilwell, the special scout camping ground. I found it a disagreeable experience, trying to sleep on hard ground with half a dozen other scouts. There was a small outdoor swimming pool, which was very heavily used, and I was horrified to see many scouts diving and swimming naked.

I think Mr Cornwall thought, also, that my wings need clipping, and to execute this plan he put me into regular boxing matches with a pleasant lad who was slightly larger than me and knew a little about boxing, which I did not. Inevitably I suffered a few sickening blows to my head each week. I still remember the sensation. I wonder whether anyone had told the scoutmaster of my previous concussion.

About this time, a conscious religious interest began to dawn in me. I went to the evening service and sat in the gallery with young people who were older than me. The minister of the church was a preacher of considerable power. He was very knowledgeable about astronomy in that Eddington and Jeans era, and this interest in astronomy has remained with me all my life. There was, too, some slightly dubious mystery about him that was never explained to me. I suppose the vastness and the scope of the Christian concept of God was beginning to dawn on me. Rev. WW had a deep fissure behind his ear, which must have been the result of a ~~cataract~~ mastoid operation. He enjoyed a friendship with my eccentric paternal grandfather, "Happy" Hammond, whom I shall mention later. I do remember one particular incident concerning Rev. WW.

My father was Missionary Secretary at the church. There was a branch at the church of the Junior Missionary Association (JMA). This consisted of children who persuaded church members to contribute a penny or tuppence a week, which they entered in their record books. The money went to Methodist missionary work overseas. If £5 was collected in a year, a silver medal was presented, with bars in subsequent years. I had persuaded the Rev. W W to contribute the requisite amount. I think 2d in his case. Once he more or less flung me half-a-crown, a vast sum for those days. I remember his wife once said to my mother, "Never pity yourself, my dear."

At this time of my life I had my first crush on a pretty young brunette called Rene. She was 12 years old. I then became aware that something was different about the male member. As Augustus John, the noted sculptor, once put it, "What begins as a fount of water changes to be a pillar of fire, and returns in age to be a fount of water." At this time my parents thought it wise to acquaint me with the facts of life. My father did so. How it must have cost him! I continued a casual acquaintance with this young lady until her family was evacuated to Wales. I only saw her once again, many years later. She had grown into a strapping physical education teacher. I was also conscious of my physique for another reason.

A few years before this time I had to have regular medically approved exercises for my chest, which was not expanding properly. I went to the local health clinic, I believe on a Saturday morning, there to be supervised by, again, a formidable nurse. I remember her injunction, "Hips firm"! I still cannot recognise the value of this posture. Whether this helped, I do not know, but I certainly began to acquire facility in physical nimbleness. This went so far as to be awarded an A1 badge at my secondary school, for facility in gym. It was a metal lapel badge with the facsimile of a heron on it. A heron was our school badge, it being near a heronry, rare in those days.

I was also interested in cars. I remember that there were two other cars in our road, apart from a firm, Morrisons, at the bottom of our road, which had two luxurious limousines for weddings and funerals. One car was owned by the father of an acquaintance, Henry Taylor. It was used for commercial travelling, in garments, I believe. It was a sturdy Morris Cowley. The other was used by Mr Pollard who lived in the last house on our side of the road. His was also used for commercial purposes. It was a baby Austin. Mr Pollard later died of double pneumonia – no antibiotics in those days.

There was also the cricket, county cricket. I had developed a particular interest in the game from the age of 11, Essex being our favoured county. My father initially took me to see them in action at the old county ground in Leyton. Later my father was always playing tennis on Saturdays, partly at least, as part of his health regime. I therefore, went on my own to the various county grounds initiated over the county at Ilford, Southend, Chelmsford, Colchester and Westcliff. At each venue two matches were played. I invariably took bread and butter, and a hard-boiled egg. I also took a bottle of Tizer, of which present day Tizer is but a pale shadow.

These were the days of Essex's great fast bowlers – Kenneth Farnes – who was killed later serving in the R AF, and Nichols, who bowled right-handed but batted left-handed. Nichols vowed that if he had learned to bowl left-handed, he would have no peer in England. There was also H.T.D. Read, known as "Hopper" Read because of the strange leap he took at the end of his run-up. A source of amusement was when a book entitled *Who's Who* was called out by the vendor. On hearing this the children among the viewers shouted "What's What"! Essex generally came third in the County Table after the giants of Yorkshire and Lancashire. Cricketers, apart from occasional charity matches, only played 16 matches of three days each year in the full season. The husband of one of my mother's cousins played for Essex. Known as "Lorry" Eastman, he was a slow medium bowler and a sound batsman. Sadly he died from cancer, aged 40. At his funeral, one wreath showed a shattered wicket, the three stumps awry.

I have recently noticed that many of these memories are concerned with bodily functions or illnesses. Presumably such incidents loom large in the life of a child. During life's ups and downs, there was always home to return to … the place of safety and security.

Chapter 2

Home

I believe that what makes a home, is the accepted basis of life and the people who compose the home. The basis of our home was the Christian faith, sincerely interpreted through Methodism and lived wonderfully according to its precepts.

My father and mother had met at East Ham Tech, and also at the local Methodist church. Dad's father was a rare eccentric who had been a valued clerk at the Liverpool Victoria Insurance Company. His wife, Maria H, had worked in the clothing trade. Their forbears were all tradesmen, boilermakers, builders, painters, etc. Many of them may well have been Methodists. My father was very different from his parents. I hate to speak of a difference in quality but I have only lately appreciated how special he was, like a rare flower blooming in a field of, say, marigolds. I *do* regret not knowing him well personally. He was nothing particular to look at, fair and stoutish. My mother came from a family that was, possibly in her father's view, slightly higher on the social ladder. He was a senior clerk in a foreign bank, although his father had been a caretaker/warehouseman to vessels in St Katherine dock. It was he, whom his children called "A saint in church but a devil at home". At the age of 14, my grandfather ran away to sea but was caught and returned home. His sister, my great aunt, was born prematurely and was carried about on a cushion. She became a Methodist Deaconess and lived a most rigorous life. She had a cold bath every morning, summer and winter. She made an annual visit to our home and heard my bedtime prayer:

> Gentle Jesus, meek and mild,
> Look upon a little child,
> Pity my simplicity,
> Suffer me to come to Thee.

She was more travelled than one might suppose, having been twice to Hawaii, where she had a relative who was a Methodist minister. She lived to the age of 90, cared for by my widowed mother. Towards the end she accused my mother of trying to poison her. I do not know if it was called Alzheimer's then.

My Methodist maternal grandmother was half German and had lovely red hair, matched by her temperament and character. My mother loved her dearly, as she did her own brother, who was killed in action during the First World War. He was a stretcher-bearer, aged 28. Possibly his death caused my grandfather's temporary insanity. However, I am in no doubt that the consequences of this tragic loss fell equally upon my mother and grandmother. Together they have been through the fire.

My grandmother, Menzler, was the daughter of a German baker who came to England and successfully opened a number of shops. His windows were broken in the First World War because of his name. He refused to change it. My grandmother was seven years older than my grandfather. He pleaded for her to marry him and was so persistent, that in the end, she accepted. She bore him one son and three daughters. The eldest daughter, her father's favourite, was very like him in character, married a businessman and lived in China. He died of peritonitis before all of their three children were grown up. My mother's younger sister was very relaxed, and placid. She had shared a bedroom with my mother, who was frequently unwell. Once my mother awoke in the night unwell. This became obvious to her younger sister, who said, "Fetch yourself a glass of water, dear!"

My paternal grandfather married at the age of 21. His wife was 20 years old. Apparently on her marriage she did not know the facts of life. They were married on April 1 and jokingly said that my father was the result. My grandfather appears to have worked normally up to the age of 50. From then on he was struck with an illness which prevented him from ever working again. The apparent cause may have been slight but enough to put an end to his career. Apparently a Methodist minister (my grandfather presumably being present), packed a meeting with his supporters to pass a particular measure. This so upset my grandfather that this nervous illness ensued. Part of it was an inability to swallow. I do not believe he and my grandmother attended church any more. He was always surrounded by a cloud of heavy shag pipe tobacco smoke. Though the future may have weighed heavily on his mind, he made the best of life in his latter years. Presumably he had a pension from his former employers, and yet he developed a flair for living economically.

He frequented a street market in a nearby town, using a tram as transport. (I remember that a child could travel a considerable distance on a half penny ticket, plucked by the conductor from his board with its rows of coloured tickets.) He trawled this market and often brought home half a pig's head or sheep's head. They would fascinate me with their half row of teeth! They had quite an amount of tasty meat. My sister, Cherry, liked my grandmother's cooking, particularly the fatty roast potatoes. My grandmother grumbled persistently, but gently at my grandfather. I remember her saying "I've been washing up for 50 years and I'm fed up with it!" She still continued. My father's younger brother, uncle Bill to us, had a considerable mathematical mind and became an actuary. Towards the end of the First World War he was completing training to become, I think, a fighter pilot. The average life of a fighter pilot was then two weeks. He was an excellent Methodist local preacher and had a stammer, like one of my mother's uncles. Perhaps my stammer was partly genetic. The third child, Kathleen, was a clerk and spent all her spare time in amateur drama, producing and acting. She was obsessed with cleanliness and seemed to spend an inordinate amount of time in the bathroom.

My father emerged from this rather strange environment. He had a natural and concealed depth of goodness that was rare. He had a keen organising mind at work and home, and exhibited the classic Christian qualities that I believe are God's gift. I only once heard him speak ill of anyone. At the same time, he never professed or paraded virtue. He was very sensitive and was terribly upset if what he believed was right was opposed. His goodness was inconspicuous – the best kind. People were amazed that he had come from such a bizarre home environment.

After the war he embraced pacifism and became deeply committed to the cause. He drove himself mercilessly, seeking to make contacts with the Germans he had fought against, and in many other practical good works. (An army captain at the age of 22, he had been engaged in leading a trench mortar battery.) He seemed reserved and I am sorry I never had a close relationship with him. I am certain that his pacifist position rubbed off on me from the age of 14; such was his influence, that when it came to my National Service I opted to work in the coal mines. (See Chapter 4.) My decision did not go down well with our caretaker at church, who was also employed at my dad's tennis club. He was a former naval man. There is no answer to these two absolutely valid positions in the Christian faith. The only position is to be absolutely tolerant of each other. (My father's hypertension – no beta-blockers then – led to his third cerebral haemorrhage and death at the age of 51.). I have really failed to describe him; a man of little casual conversation, whom I unconsciously loved and appreciated.

As an aside here, I could mention that his eccentric father, who came to be known as "Happy" Hammond, was the aforementioned unusual friend of the great preacher Rev. WW. They went to football matches together. "Happy" Hammond also kept aviaries of caged foreign birds and grew prize chrysanthemums. He, like my dad, had little small talk.

My mother's fiery temperament has greatly diminished. Much of it may well have been the result of an encounter which changed her life. One day she hurried home to her mother after a Sunday service and said, excitedly, "I've given my heart to Jesus." Her mother replied "Splendid, but I shall expect to see results in your living." She and my father were married in 1918, while he was still an army officer. He would certainly have burnt his uniform (which was infested with lice), when he came on leave, and bought a new one. He, incidentally, had been awarded the Military Cross. He said afterwards that they handed them out with the rations. I heard later that he was the last to leave when the Germans captured a town and he had to ride a horse for the first time in his life.

At first my parents lived in rooms in east London while a small house was being built for them in South Woodford. My father must have accumulated money from his officer's pay. There their first child, Cherry, was born. The house was called "Cherrydene". They soon joined the local Methodist church in Derby Road which became the centre of our lives, even though my father was absorbed in his career. He wanted to progress at his work in insurance and working late at night, drove himself until he had passed all the insurance examinations. I do not know whether this contributed to his very high blood pressure, virtually incurable in those days. He also served as a church steward, a responsible and demanding post.

Money always had to be carefully considered in our family life. My pocket money was two pence per week but I was also allowed two pence for a weekly "tupenny blood" comic, *The Modern Boy,* which had futuristic adventures. I was allowed also money for sweets, generally two ounces for one penny. I generally went for some kind of liquorice or acidic boiled sweets. I ate far more than was good for my teeth. With regard to dentists, I had a pronounced under hung jaw, and our dentist persuaded my parents to allow me to have a solid silver cap over my bottom teeth. It cost £5, nearly half my father's weekly wage! I don't really think it made any difference. The one occasion when my mother had a good spend out was when her uncle J left her a legacy, I believe, of £50. Oh joy! She bought my brother a bicycle and a tricycle for me. For herself she bought a grey squirrel fur coat and a Clarice Cliff dinner service. I still remember snuggling up to that coat during church services.

Before Rev. WW became our minister, Rev. H was in charge. He smoked a pipe. One of our oldest members, Mr Ockleford, who sported a long yellowish beard, took Rev.

H to task for smoking. This was well before the dangers of smoking were appreciated. When this somewhat formidable minister demurred, Mr O said, "Truth is 'ard brother 'ingley, truth is 'ard", Rev. H replied, "I'll tell you what Mr O ... if you cut off your beard, I'll give up my pipe." Neither happened. On another occasion there was a church meeting with the minister Rev. W. He had recently returned from being the superintendent minister of a large number of African ministers and churches, so he was, I imagine, somewhat dictatorial. Superintendent ministers in Methodism have wide organising and executive powers. Some of the members did not agree with the superintendent's plans and one of them actually called out "We're not your bloody niggers, you know." And this in a Methodist meeting! This was the same man who infuriated my mother by frequently giving her a large hug after the morning service. She was not given to effuse displays of affection.

The church had a large, very active and effective congregation with plenty of people of all ages. There were house groups, a strong pacifist and socialist element, an enthusiastic junior church, drama and literary sections, and others I cannot remember. Sadly, I had to leave this community when I was evacuated at the age of 14. The Sunday School used *Songs of Praise* as their hymnbook. It was then recently published. I know by heart many of the hymns now. I use it every day in my devotions. My father gave to this church the absolute commitment that he gave to everything. My parents grew to be ever more committed and devoted to each other. With my birth a larger property became necessary.

We moved, therefore, to Empress Avenue, to a four-bedroomed house, which was terraced. I have described its garden previously. It had a coal chute at the front, down which poured the appropriate load of anthracite. It then lay glittering in the mysterious cellar below the house. It was used to fuel the stove which heated our dining room. Washing was done by hand in the scullery, which had a copper. Stained or extra dirty clothing was rubbed on a washing board. A large wringer stood in the corner with wooden rollers. Irons were heated on the gas. I shared a bed with my brother until he had an operation for peritonitis in a London hospital. The appendix was removed just in time. For years afterwards I feared I would get the same disease. Every twinge on the left hand side was suspicious.

We had a cupboard full of toys in the kitchen. They were all lost when the house was destroyed by a flying bomb, the V1. For some odd reason there were few books in the house – I had to read my limited collection several times over!

The great social occasion was Sunday tea, to which was invited all available friends and relatives and any church friends that were isolated in colleges. The table was magnificently loaded with culinary wonders. I once demolished almost a plateful of Jaffa biscuits, while my brother, unsuccessfully, pleaded for more.

After Sunday lunch we always had family prayers where we all knelt in front of armchairs in the drawing room. I found it unreal and embarrassing. We then had a piece of wholesale chocolate bars, whipped cream walnuts, crunchies and other delicious confections. For breakfast I always had egg, bacon and bread soaked in bacon fat, except on Sundays, when it was sausage and tomatoes. In winter I sometimes had porridge with milk and syrup. I was not much interested in other meals. For sweet I generally had cereals with milk and sugar. I did, however, like boiled potatoes and peas ... I was happy at home. I remember a notice on the inside of the bathroom door.

> The lease of this well-watered spot is short.
> Extension can't be got,
> Haste then, for in ten minutes more,
> The next will thunder at the door!

Our home was enlivened from time to time with visits from our cousins. My mother's younger sister, Florence (aunt Floss), lived in Belgium, very near Brussels, I think. Her husband, uncle Wilfred, was manager of the Belgian branch of the "O" Insurance Company. They were much wealthier than we were. Wilfred eventually became manager of the entire insurance operation. The two elder Leng boys, there were eventually five in all, were boarders at the minor public school at Chigwell, which I so happily avoided. On their days off they came to visit us with large empty tuck boxes. These were refilled with some of Rose's excellent large cakes, and perhaps, her wonderful ginger bread. The elder boy, Tony, became a language master at Malvern public school. Donald, the younger cousin, was completely different to Tony in nearly every way. In adolescence he became greatly interested in the Christian faith and the Bible in particular. This affected him mentally. His mother, aunt Floss, said that when she saw his Bibles come out she knew that trouble was brewing. Donald later became a clerk in London and joined the Plymouth Brethren. He married Olive Branch, who was from the same denomination. Their elder son did not follow his parent's way and was befriended by my sister Cherry at Oxford. He is now dead, pre-deceasing his parents. Uncle Wilfred sometimes stayed with us when he visited London from Belgium. I find him difficult to describe.

Once, I remember, he had gone alone to the lesser of our two local cinemas, the Plaza. On the next morning he, apparently, had been bitten by a flea and said he had bought "a sixpenny cinema seat and attracted a sixpenny flea". I believe I may have gone to the Plaza on Saturday mornings for their special children's programmes, but not once did I attract fleas. I was a little in awe of him. In his 50s he contracted a dreadful disease that caused calcium to infect his bones and heart. He died in sadness. Aunt Floss was dark, warm and cuddly, with a honeyed voice. I liked her.

The other family who visited were those of my widowed aunt Edith, she who was so like her father and his favourite daughter. The death of her husband had left her in very poor financial circumstances when she returned to England. She was helped considerably by my grandfather who eventually bought a pleasant modern house to accommodate her family and himself. The house was in Buckhurst Hill and the road had the delightful name, Little Plucketts Way. Aunt Edie did have some regular financial support from my hard-pressed father and uncle Wilfred. Aunt Edie's elder son, Arthur, was among the handsomest men I have ever met, strong aquiline features and piercing light blue eyes. After casting around, rather listlessly, for a career, he joined the RAF and became a fighter pilot and "one of the few" who saved England from a German invasion. Later he was responsible for training Polish men as fighter pilots. He did not visit us with his brother and sister, being occupied on duty. Once I was staying with aunt Edie, after her father had died, and Arthur was there. Having adopted my father's pacifist views at the age of 14, I had the temerity to ask Arthur how he felt about killing enemy pilots. He looked down at me with his piercing blue eyes, containing an inner contempt for this cheeky whippersnapper, and said, "It's them or you". On the one occasion I have met him afterwards, at his brother's funeral service, I think he carefully avoided noticing me. Mind you, I was wearing my "dog collar"! Now aged 89, and with serious bladder problems, he cares for his blind wife of 94 devotedly.

Roland, the younger boy, was very much an open-air lad. His great watchword for all that he did in physical activities, particularly cycling, was "to keep fit". Unkindly I have occasionally wondered in later years "To keep fit ... What for"? He had ginger hair like his younger sister, Enid, whom I liked. At times this assembly of cousins met together, apart from the adults. I, of course, tried to establish an equality with them. They clearly regarded me as a nuisance who had to be tolerated. Roland was operated on for bowel cancer in his late 50s. Sadly this was too late and he died, presumably of liver cancer, 22 years ago, at the age of 63. His wife is much younger than he, to the extent that she is now four years younger than I. She is the organist of the ancestral Derby Road Methodist Church. All this came to an end at the outbreak of the Second World War when I was evacuated with my school, for fear of the bombing that might ensue. People had appreciated the terrible reality of Guernica. Soon after my father's insurance firm, the AMP Society, were evacuated to a very large mansion in extensive grounds, full of whortleberry bushes, at Hindhead in Surrey, a beautiful site near to the well-known country feature, Devil's Punchbowl.

Chapter 3

School, Evacuation & Teacher Training

This heading might seem strange, but we were (from time to time), evacuated from school premises to various places around the country during the war. This chapter is about my most remembered experiences.

When I first went secondary school it was with trepidation. I had heard dark talk of bullying and kindred unpleasant things. When we "the new ticks" arrived in the playground, a group of us were approached by a menacing posse. No members of staff were present. Among our all male group, was a boy called Wagstaff. He was the smallest boy present. His face was covered in freckles, and mercy on us, he wore short trousers! He had evidently been recognised by the posse as the brother of a prefect who was a strong disciplinarian. What an opportunity, they thought, as they approached us, their eyes fixed menacingly on their "prey". But lo and behold, little Wagstaff smote one of the posse smartly on the nose. They slipped away, surely having suffered a big blow to their reputation.

Life was quite enjoyable in this autumn of 1936. It was a new experience, coming from the male section of a council school. As usual I unconsciously courted popularity. The girls, seemingly more gifted and indifferent to us, usually came first in most of the studies. I did seem to be well liked among the boys. I cannot think why. I did not seem to be unduly pressured in my work, probably because I did as little as I could. I was starting to realise my limitations. Any subject, apart from PT, English and it allies, history and geography, was very unattractive to me. I learnt French by rote, but could never remember the vocabulary. Apart from simple arithmetic, I could not, and never have, grasped algebra. I could grasp the logic of geometry but that grasp was painfully slow. I was not academic and was gratified, but still puzzled, why I was, at the age of 13, transferred to a class called "4 Special", presumably for high fliers. Here I actually came first in geography, a dizzy height indeed. Staff had obviously been warned of my impertinences and kept a sharp hold on me. Our form teacher was a young and immensely popular geography teacher called Mr R. A few years later he was killed by a British tank.

I particularly enjoyed PT, having apparently some facility in it. Even the fearsome PT master, a man with one eye and few words except those of command, seemed to think so. I have previously stated that I was even awarded the A1 badge that had a heron facsimile on it. This was the only school honour I ever gained.

My transport to and from school was by a small 24" wheel bicycle, four times a day, in journeys of perhaps two to three miles. I survived safely in those days of limited traffic. My worst experience was when my front wheel was caught in a disused train rail. Even then I was not thrown off the saddle. Mr K, a master and member of the Peace Pledge Union, particularly attracted me. I used to wait for him near the school entrance as he cycled home. He successfully survived, what to him must have been, a very awkward situation.

From time to time our school put on dramatic shows supervised by our large, sixty-ish, music and art teacher, known universally as "Spud" Parker. The time came when he needed a singer from the lower school to fulfil a principal role. I knew I had a clear voice but, still shaken by the debacle at the Methodist Circuit Eisteddfod, I flatly refused. At a further show I was shoehorned to play the part of Adolph Hitler with my hair drawn down and to stride about the stage shouting absolute nonsense and "Heil Hitlering" every few moments. Of course, whether it was intended to ridicule the dark menace on the horizon, or to slap down the pert nuisance, I do not know. I certainly had a sore throat afterwards. We also had a bazaar to raise school funds. Bravely daring, I painfully worked two pieces of alabaster into primitive faces. They did not sell. One of the staff at the school was a kind and efficient physics teacher. For some reason this pleasant man was "ragged" mercilessly. Stylised facsimiles of his face were chalked everywhere. On recollection I think it must have been an eruption of unadulterated evil. I hope he was not destroyed, as teachers can be in this wretched situation. More of this will come to the fore when I talk about my own career in teaching. (See Chapter 5.)

Next it will be as well to think about the Second World War and my evacuation with a considerable part of my school. Our first journey ended in Chelmsford, where we spent a fortnight. From this point on, and in years to come, it dawned on me with increasing conviction that the world was not my oyster, and that I had to be accommodated in the plans and purposes of other people. I was eventually billeted at the home of the deputy headmaster of the local grammar school, who a week or so previously, had married the church secretary. I felt very clearly that I was not welcome. Moreover, I suspect that the rather fierce gentleman might have been warned that he was in me, nursing a viper in his bosom. I only dared open my mouth twice. Therefore, I was thankful that our school moved to Maldon on the Essex coast, where a group of us were billeted in the Youth Hostel.

A couple ran the hostel, principally the wife I imagine, with all its catering, etc. The lady was pleasant and motherly, but whom it was foolish to cross. Her husband was a man of limited speech who thought that the best way to deal with our German foes was to "spray acid on the b … s". One day the butter provided at one of our meals was rancid and I could not eat it. News of this reached the lady of the house and I was in the "doghouse" for some time. Later she discovered that the butter *was* rancid, and came and apologised handsomely to me in a big way. Bless her.

Throughout my future schooling I was wonderfully sustained by the local Methodist churches. Several of the members among them took a particular and loving interest in us and I can never thank them sufficiently. They were my lifeline and showed me what Christian love was. I joined the Methodist church as a member about halfway through my schooldays.

Nevertheless, around the age of 16 I endured long periods of mental misery. One of our teachers, a fierce Scottish man, I think, saw my condition and called at my billet a number of times to help me with my Latin, and incidentally, cheered my spirits with his gruff kindness. Perhaps the Latin was a pastoral excuse, as it must have been clear how hopeless I was at that language. Someone, by a stroke of genius, had organised my transfer to a Methodist family of early middle age who had no children. I was treated like a son. The husband was in charge of boilers at some industrial firm and was one of the best men I have ever met. I believe he was of a Baptist background but his obviously vital work prevented him from attending worship. He was like a father to me, reflecting to me the qualities of my own father. Such profound unconscious goodness cannot be described. He also introduced me to the works of Thomas Hardy. His wife was a little bird-like lady who was also wonderfully good to me, as was her mother, who lived with us. Between them I believe they melted away my mental distress and hopefully some of my obtuse self-centredness. After I left school to go to teacher training college, Mrs S, my hostess, kept my school cap. We visited the family when our children were young, wrote regularly to them, and then, one day, received a reply, "not known at this address". They are surely in glory.

Whilst at Maldon it dawned on me, for the first time, how little I was likely to pass my Matriculation exam. I had never worked conscientiously. So, I set about vainly to put things, particularly French, to rights. I really did try, but all to no avail. I thought I should fail because a pass was necessary in maths, which apart from arithmetic and simple geometry, I could make little sense of. English, history and geography were no problem. Then the dreaded mathematics exam day came. Time rushed by and within the last five minutes of the exam I managed to get a geometry theorem proven. On the day of the results, Margaret, one of the more attractive of the gifted girls in our class, was spreading successful results. "Hammond, you've got Matric," she said. I still regard the pass in maths as well nigh miraculous. Next, of course, we went on to Higher School Certificate studies. I was engaged in English, history, geography and, mercy on us, French. On explaining the situation I was allowed to drop French. This meant I could never get my Higher School Certificate. The geography mistress complained that my essays did not reflect a higher content from other books. (The trouble was that there were no other books available.) After the first year of the sixth form I saw no hope of any meaningful future career. In fact the future looked very bleak. I ought to include the strange, almost final occasion at school.

The headmaster came down, I think primarily to speak with Mr R, our former class teacher in 4 Special, resplendent in officer's uniform; I went to the school offices hoping for a word from him but he took no notice of me and went into the headmaster's study. Afterwards the Headmaster came out and buttonholed me. "Hammond," he said, "I want you to go back to Wanstead and be head boy." Most of the school had then returned to its Wanstead site. I tried to explain to him that my Christian faith did not include that option. He did not appear to understand free churchmanship.

Then notice was received that places were available on a teacher-training course. Teachers were urgently needed; teachers of any kind. Places were available for 17-year-olds to take a two year course. The options were: to remain for two years, or leave after the first year and return for a completing year after completing National Service. I chose the former. The course was at the prestigious Goldsmith's College, which had been evacuated to Nottingham. The interview was by a doctor who had obviously never taught, but had some connection with Goldsmith's College. Naturally I stammered badly. Somehow I gained a place. Indeed they were calling in "the halt and the lame"! At Goldsmith's I learned little about the art of teaching. That was learned, painfully, later. I enjoyed the educational theory and the history lectures. There was no relationship between the educational lectures and the teaching I gave for 24 years. It was a truism that educational lecturers and supervisors had never actually experienced the average classroom. Probably their practical understanding was limited to a good-class grammar school. It is different now.

Dr Rideout, the history lecturer, had ill-fitting false dentures that chattered independently of his mouth and words. He was not young and I have wondered whether he had taught principally in higher institutions. We were, perhaps, a quiet run into retirement. He gave very wide-ranging lectures and I liked him very much. We eventually had to produce a major thesis. I had no idea, at the age of 17, how to go about this. I decided on a Spanish notable called de Mariaga. I could not find any relevant books except the major work about him, so my "thesis" consisted of large chunks of this book with some attempt at interpretation in between. It was passed. Dr Rideout, greatly daring I think, sometimes included slightly outré stories. One I remember. A queue of people were urgently in need of the toilet but there was someone using it. Dr Rideout was second in line. He said to the lady in front "Courage madam, I hear paper." I could personally appreciate this, as my inner workings have always been unreliable, until recent years.

I enjoyed the bookbinding and carpentry classes. The lecturer, Mr Windle, was extremely friendly and informal. I actually rebound two books and made a wooden box. I remember his written comment was along the lines "A good result after unsparing effort". It was a fair comment. I can generally produce a presentable effort after a very long time. One education lecturer, who had learned of my beliefs, confronted me by expounding the secular view on the foolishness of faith. I believe that faith is entirely a matter of faith; it is a trusting relationship that is not based on empirical things. However, I think it was very unprofessional of him to approach me in this personal way, and I was too young and inexperienced to take it up with a higher authority.

School practices were interesting experiences. I was placed in a little country council school out in the sticks. The head was a little dried up man who spoke somewhat salaciously of girls being "ripe for motherhood". I was drafted to a class whose teacher was suffering from a dreadful genetic disease which attacks the bone structure, and was turning a fine upstanding man from normality into an ape-like creature. He was bearing this horrible fate bravely. There was a dark man, African or West Indian, on the small staff, who was absolutely didactic on historical facts and would not tolerate any difference expressed by me. I kept quiet. The experience left me wondering about life and the world; I saw little relation between college and real life.

I was right "out of the swim" in the social and student power centres at the college. I did join the Student Christian Movement (SCM), and it being very small, was made president. There was a large and flourishing Christian fundamentalist organisation, the Christian Union, which was an anathema to my way of thinking, even at that tender age. The best part of the SCM was the lectures and short conferences organised for students. There we heard notable ministers and writers in their younger years. Among them was David Jenkins, who in his formative years became a theologian, and religious writer on Congregationalism. I drank it all in, along with my lessons during the first year of training. While many of my male colleagues left after the first year (to go into the Forces), I preferred to stay on and complete the course. That second year was the most momentous in my life, for in it I met my future wife, dear Hilda.

I went along to the first SCM meeting of the new term and noticed three girls sitting near the front. One was busily knitting; the other two were obviously her friends. The first girl took my eye and that was the beginning. I attached myself to the group and apparently for some time they could not decide who I was interested in. I suppose they gradually became aware. One, Olive G, has remained our lifelong friend. The other we have lost touch with. The rest of that year is virtually a blur. We had some café meals together. In those days it was reconstituted egg on toast or beans on toast but it was mostly spent getting to know each other. I can't remember if I actually proposed marriage during this time but I was certainly accepted when I did. Happy me! I left the training with a Teaching Certificate specialising in history. Blessings on you Dr Rideout. I have a shrewd suspicion that the pass standard in those days was generous, to say the least. I was only 18 and there was a desperate shortage of teachers.

Chapter 4

The Coalmines
1944 – 1947

So, now I had to "do" my National Service. I did not fancy sticking a bayonet in someone (more tolerable to be stuck like a pig myself), and there was an option to work in a coal mine. I knew that every possible ton of coal was needed for the economy – no thought of global warming then – I doubt the phrase was even known. Furthermore, I had deeply absorbed my father's Christian pacifism, and further, was rather a miserable physical specimen to be of any use in a fighting unit.

The interview to place those who were called up was degrading. Everyone was individually called up in front of a doctor, stark naked, and were ordered to walk around like cattle in a market. I felt like an animal being examined. The doctor was of a particularly military appearance; not one to offer sympathy and understanding. In fact, I think I caught a look of contempt as he regarded the specimen before him. He did not improve my appreciation of military discipline.

So I was bound for the coal mines with only the vaguest idea of what it would be like. The special train was crowded with both Bevin boys, who were compelled to work in the mines (their numbers coming up in a lottery), and those like myself, who had chosen to work in coal mining. Our compartment was full of raucous company and one particular man seemed drawn towards me like a magnet. He was even slighter than I was. His name was Tom C. He was a Salvationist, aged 35, and an excellent lay preacher. We wrote to each other once a year until he reached the age of 80, when he died. He married a Salvationist girl from Nottingham, of about his own age. I think the authorities looked at him and decided that he was not suitable for physical work. He was a skilled clerk so they employed him in that capacity in the Coal Board Office, where I am sure he benefited the coal mining industry more than the rest of us put together. Our training consisted of giving us a trip down to the pit bottom, a huge whitewashed hall with walls of brick. One side was a cul-de-sac; the other, the start of tunnels that led into the working part of the mine.

Make no mistake, the miners, apart from a very few mavericks, were roughly kind and helped you all they could. The major difference was that when they spoke, every other word was a four-letter word. It meant absolutely nothing and I think they were a little puzzled that I did not use that word. Their odd use of language was called "pit talk".

The miners, at this time, were just about emerging from a period when they had been exploited by private mine owners and possibly had been sacked at will, over making little profit for the mine owners. Now expansion was the word, with new seams being opened and the coal production each hour being written on the side of the tubs (little coal trucks). They still remembered, I think, their war cry in their tussle with the mine owners:

> Eight hours work, eight hours play,
> Eight hour sleep and eight bob a day.

Incidentally, I first saw the surrender of the German

armies, VE day, written on the side of a tub. The first few months were spent in pulling the tubs out of the cages so they could be added to the train of them going towards the coalfaces. It was hard work but it toughened us up a little to meet the next challenge.

My first lodging was interesting. It was in a home where the husband was much older than his wife. When he saw an Indian he insisted they addressed him as "Sahib". He had worked in India. *Ugh!* His wife was stout, pale, with a moon face and had pale ginger hair. They had two wire-haired terriers, whom I am sure consumed our meat ration, while we had preserved meats like salami. She read my intimate letters to Hilda. One day her husband told me to leave. I was pleased to do so. I suppose she had read some derogatory comment about her in my letters. Later lodgers looked in her rent book, which was hopelessly in debt.

My next lodging was in a warm-hearted household with jolly Freda and her husband who was an epileptic and could only work intermittently on the coalface. Their prime lodger was a fisher lad from the north east. I think he also worked on the coalface. We liked Freda a great deal. She was a good sport and made the very best she could out of our limited rations. She made good gravy. We generally had fried cheese for breakfast. Cheese was the only extra ration the miners had, 8 ounces each week. I think the public had 1 ounce. We put this cheese in between slices of the excellent wartime bread. This was our "snap". Later, whilst working in the mines, I used to buy cooked beetroot to add a little zest to the midday meal. We ate out of newspapers to try to preserve some degree of cleanliness. One day, while working at the pit bottom with the tubs, a miner, coming early from the coalface, handed me his "snap". It had bacon in it. Oh bliss. Oh joy! But there were times when our joy was marred by tragedy.

One day my Baptist mate, working near me hauling tubs off the cage at the pit bottom, mistimed his footing and his thigh was crushed. He said he prayed all the way to hospital. He was invalided out of the mines, and I believe, received £100 compensation. I have recently tried to contact him, but with no success as yet. He must be at least 80, like myself. After completing his National Service he went into teaching and lived in Kent, near Mersham. I remember that somehow I was able to go to his 21 birthday party. When I awoke there was a magnificent chorus of birdsong. This was quite unlike the industrial village where our Gedling Pit was situated.

My day consisted of getting myself up at 4 o'clock in the morning to cycle to work. One morning I did not have a functioning front lamp. I was stopped by a pleasant policeman who gave me a summons. I had to pay a fine. I thought afterwards, that he was over zealous. Surely a warning would have sufficed. Once at the pit I changed into my working clothes – unwashed ragged clothes – that were hauled up on the end of a rope near the ceiling. Then we tramped across to the pithead and climbed the steel stairs to where the cages came up from the pit bottom. The cages were wooden structures with open iron gates. We crammed into a cage and the gateman pushed in as many people as he could and forced the bolt shut. I preferred to be in the inside of the cage as the gate was frail and there was a drop of 440 yards to the pit bottom. I did not care for the gap between the ground and the cage. It would have been a long way to drop. The cage descended at a dizzy speed to the pit bottom. After all the men were down, the cages had two tubs full of coal every time they reached the surface.

My worst experience in the pit, was one time, when I was "riding" the cage up to the surface. The winding man applied too much speed to the great cable and the cage jumped up beyond the rope and then fell like a stone. One of the other miners was the crack miner at our coalface. When we reached the surface, this man went to the winding house and spoke a few very choice words to the winding man. I thought my end had come and I would end up a mess on the pit bottom.

The coalface is where the cutting of coal is achieved. It broadly consists of a main tunnel, called a gate, which is joined at its end by two tunnels at right angles. These are the two coalfaces. In them the shiny coal is clearly visible, 3 foot high. The coal is undercut each 24 hours to a yard depth. The cycle is as follows:

On the day shift (6.00 am to 2.00 pm) the coal is cut down and removed. On the afternoon shift (2.00 pm to 10.00 pm), the new coalface is undercut by a very heavy machine, called a cutter, which is drawn along the face on a cable, the cutter drawn along by an engine at the end of the coalface, and then holes are drilled along the coalface. On the night shift the pit props, made of wood or steel, which are erected by the miner to support the roof where he has removed the coal, are taken down and the portable belt running along the coalface are moved forward. The area behind the coalface is left bare of support and collapses. This is known as the "goaf". Each coalface miner has a yardage of coal to remove, usually 8 or 10 yards, depending on his skill and experience. The official in charge of each face is the shot firer. He charges each of the drilled holes with an explosive cartridge, fixes a wire into each one and presses his electric battery. This blows some of the coal from the coalface with a resounding thump. Everyone has previously moved out of danger. The coal is thus partly blown down. The job of a miner is to cut down the rest of the coal on his stint and load it onto the belt running along the face. This would consist of 10 cubic yards of coal, several tons. Coal itself is not heavy. At the gate the two moving belts unload their coal into a belt running for some yards up the gate to a loading end. At this point the coal falls into tubs run under it and then attached by a Smallman clip on to a moving wire above a rail track and carried up the gate towards the pit bottom. The gate is extended on the night shift to the new position of the coalface.

From the pit bottom I was transferred to the loading end on number two face, the faces numbers two and three, being the most productive ones in our Gedling Pit. The most menial job on the loading end is to work in the spillage hole, on the far side of the empty tubs coming under the end, to keep the ground clear of coal falling off the belt. It involves shovelling solidly for the eight-hour shift, not as backbreaking as it sounds, as there is a knack to shovelling. Then one graduates to operating the handle which allows each empty tub under the loading end. This, again, is a knack, as operating it too loosely allows the empty tubs to push, still empty, under the belt. The weight of perhaps 20 empty tubs needs careful control. From this occupation the worker graduates up the gate to control the movement of the empty tubs down the hill to the loader end. This is a one-man job, solitary work in complete darkness, apart from the dim, heavy, miner's lamp swinging from one's belt. The movement is controlled by removing the Smallman clip and jamming the wheels of the front tub by a thick piece of wood. Stop and start signals are passed to the end of the gate by an overhead wire. Once, before I was used to the work, I could not stop the tubs and a very amiable local supervisor came down and exploded in a shower of pit language. It was the *de rigueur* method of responding to inefficiency. I was forgiven speedily. My final promotion was back to the pit bottom, controlling the movement of the larger new tubs that were being introduced to facilitate production. My final work at the pit was to be a steel checker.

A casual acquaintance of mine, a steel checker, wanted to have me working with him. After an interview with the pit manager this was permitted. This was to go along the empty coalface on the afternoon shift and poke about in the goaf for any steel pit props that, in his hurry, a miner might have left. I then had to mark on the roof with chalk the position where it was found. The miner was then fined ten shillings, a considerable sum then. A special steel tipped stick was provided to poke through the dirt and tap on the steel prop. I always felt rather mean, "a bosses' man". The shot firers and officials carried a special hand lamp that projected a beam. Steel checkers had the same type. When miners saw the beam of these lamps, they were instinctively very cautious. I suppose it reminded them of the bad old days.

The lodgings we went to, after Freda's, were very different. A shrivelled-looking old lady, who lived apparently on tea and cigarettes, ran them. She had previously run a boarding house at Herne Bay. She occasionally would hark back to the days when she had been a daring knickerbocker girl – presumably in Edwardian times. She kept Khaki Campbell brown ducks, a very useful resource in those times. The highlight of the week, there, was a splendid Sunday dinner with all the trimmings, using up all our weekly rations I would judge. Dessert was a slice of her delicious fruitcake. I once had the temerity to ask for a second slice. My request was unsuccessful.

I made furniture during my spare time. For some time I had been working on the under structure of a dining table and it was eventually put to good use when we were married. (I bought the oak locally and gradually fashioned it into the necessary shapes.) I used the remaining pieces of the same wood to make small bits of furniture, which we still have today. I was also studying for London University Certificate in Religious Knowledge. In spite of a daily shower after each shift down the mines, one could never really get clean. I shudder to think of the dirty washing I sent home each week to my mother.

Chapter 5

Teaching

In December 1947 I applied for work in Essex; I wanted to be near where my mother now lived. I lived with my mother until my marriage to Hilda, in August 1948. (My great-aunt Emma had now died. My mother lived well beyond my father. She died from secondary cancers, more than 25 years after her mastectomy during her 40s. In her final hour she must have been heavily sedated, because her green eyes could not see. With her last breath, she whispered to us [three children], "Goodbye, my dears." Her corneas were given away as a donation.)

The teaching post offered me was in Dagenham, where the great Ford Motor Works was situated. Sometimes I cycled the 7 or 8 miles to work, or alternatively, travelled by bus.

I did not know what to expect. Most of the experienced staff had fairly recently left the Armed Forces and were also fairly street wise. The only lady on the staff was very capable but close to retirement. We got on very well together and I inherited from her the school library, and I think, the school magazine. I was very much, at 23, the youngest member of staff. I truly had little idea of maintaining class discipline and had a hard time establishing order. One over zealous school governor came round the school one day and complained to the headmaster that my classroom was like a smoking concert.

Gradually I learnt the rudiments of establishing order and getting some education done.

The first rule was to have an invariable routine, an effective one in that, when you teach a class for the first time, you initiate this routine. My favourite was for everyone to stand behind their desks, myself included, and then to sit and commence work. This is particularly effective when a class first comes from junior school to secondary school. The second is the use of strong eye contact with any child involved in mild misdemeanour. The third can be to never shout. Eventually a combination of these techniques became effective and I had a more comfortable time teaching. To my responsibilities were added the charge of the school cricket team, which involved after school matches and training sessions. (For the latter there was a small payment that was very welcome.)

One of the staff, a very large Welshman who used to play for one of the London Welsh teams, saw Hilda when she came to a cricket match when, I believe, our school cricket team was entertaining that from another school. He later referred to Hilda as "a little filly". I was very annoyed but did not take the matter up; he could have flattened me. He used to wash his games kit at school and hang it to dry on the staffroom radiator. He was married to the headmistress of the girl's school, which was situated on the first floor of our rather bleak 30s building. I never saw any female staff or girl pupils in the three years I taught at this school. In retrospect, this seems extraordinary. This Welsh teacher regularly used a piece of lath to keep order in his classes. I'm sure he never needed it.

When I took charge of them (the school cricket team) we won the local school championship. I waxed poetic in reporting this in the school magazine. (I seemed in these responsibilities to have considerably more than any other member of staff.) Could the new boy have been put upon? This later became true in my final school where I taught for 20 years. My flight of words in the magazine concerned erecting a building of fame through the labours of my lads.

The staff kept me well slapped down. The more experienced of them kept me well in my place at first but eventually adjusted to this "new boy". They had probably never encountered a newly trained teacher. For example, when I left my bicycle outside the staffroom, it being the only safe place in the school, they put it outside the staffroom window. My weekly wage was a little over £5, brought round in a brown envelope by the school secretary.

During this time I visited Hilda and her family as often as possible. They lived in Kingston. If I stayed overnight, Hilda had a bed in the small bedroom adjoining a larger bedroom. Her father and I shared this bedroom which led out from it. Chaperoning was very thorough in those days. Hilda had one sister, M, an attractive tomboy with her mother's great blue eyes and splendid curly blonde hair. She would have been about 14 to 15. On my first visit she plonked herself on my lap, to her mother's considerable displeasure, and was rapidly removed. Her father was a very gifted man who had spent the First World War in the trenches and survived. He was afterwards an infantryman with the Black and Tans in Ireland. Then having obtained employment in the Civil Service, he rose, eventually, to one of its most responsible jobs, writing replies to MPs and other's questions and comments for the minister of Labour. He was a very strong character in all respects. His religious faith was akin to unitarianism and he did not believe in life after death. He was an expert on Dickens and was a faithful member of the Adult School Movement, a quasi-religious organisation which met every Sunday. A life-long pipe smoker, he gave up immediately, when the price of tobacco became too high, his distress mitigated by the chewing of liquorice. Hilda's mother, Rose, was a delightful person and a skilled tailor. She was reserved and economical in speech and was an excellent plain cook. I grew to love her. Hilda's sister Margaret, and her husband, Fred, are life-long friends, very probably our principal friends. They have a son and a daughter. Fred is very gifted. He has gained two degrees, a BA and MA, and is knowledgeable in a number of other fields. After our wedding in August 1948, I remained in that school for two years before leaving in 1950.

By some extraordinary coincidence all the experienced staff (except two), died within about two years after I left, including the headmaster, who had been promoted to a larger school in Gidea Park, Romford. Of the two who still remained alive, one was the deputy head, a rather colourless, though very amiable man in his late 40s. I guess he may have obtained this promotion because it being war-time, there was no other permanent teacher available. The other, a spare rubicund man in his mid 30s, once told me that an older boy, Tommy Taylor, confided to him that I walked about the school like "King Tut". Not, I think, the height of professional conduct.

I remember he [the rubicund man] came up to me [before Hilda and I were married] and asked, *sotto voce*, what Lodge I belonged to. It transpired that he was a Mason and thought I was also. I think, also, he tried to give me the Mason's special handshake. I was astonished. Later, when he was promoted to headmaster of a junior school, he had returned to renew his acquaintances, and knowing that I would need furniture for my marital home, tried to sell me a very well-worn bed settee for £10, nearly two weeks wages for me at that time. After consultation with Hilda we politely declined. We were not that green, even 57 years ago. It was a blessing that I had managed to save £100 during my time in mining. I did not smoke or drink, which was helpful. This saving meant we could afford a decent bedroom suite from the onset. It was a time of limited choice, when furniture manufactured in Czecho-Slovakia was virtually the only easily available brand on the market. Eventually we decided to purchase our own property by mortgage and we found a suitable one on the borders of Dagenham for £1,500. What we did not know was that our neighbour was a street trader in Romford market.

Two years after our marriage I applied for a position at a new school being built on the outskirts of Romford, at Harold Hill. This was to accommodate the children of a housing clearance in east London. It transpired that the school was not yet completed, so I was drafted for a year to a junior school for which I had no training or experience. The Welsh headmaster, Mr H, seemed to be always guarding his back. This did not endear him to me. The class comprised six to seven-year-olds of mixed ability, and I tried to cope without too much difficulty. The main trouble was a child called Christobel Johnson. She would run home at every opportunity. I was not in a position to attempt to stop her. I had to immediately report each occasion to the headmaster, who tut-tutted, and assigned the blame to me. I felt it futile to argue on the matter. I did not get a good written testimonial from this headmaster.

In 1953 my new school was finally completed, and a luxurious structure it was! It was designed by a notable architect and cost £250,000 – I think it would cost £20,000,000 now! The staff was assembled from most parts of Britain. At first, for about two years, it was a mixed school but girls and boys were in separate classes. We assembled together with our recently appointed headmaster. He was a short, quietly spoken Oxford graduate, who came from Burnley. He managed a motley crew of staff and the pupils from a London house clearance, expertly and admirably. I respected him immensely and always addressed him as "Sir". I think his life was sullied by difficulties of debt, and knowledge of this may have hampered his chances of being the headteacher of the combined boys and girls school when we had to amalgamate due to the falling number of children on the estate. The headmistress of the girls' school obtained that position. Our mathematics head of department, a rare post then, as now, was quite intractable about not cooperating with her and I wonder whether her early retirement a few years later might have been due to this. I found her very pleasant, if a little uncertain about how to lead the men in our new combined staff. When I officially retired after 20 years on the staff of this school (there was normally a staff meeting at the departure of long-serving staff), I saw fit to give this lady a kiss. I think this astonished those among the staff who did not cooperate with her for reasons I could never understand, and further lowered, perhaps, their opinion of me. I am certain that the two who would not cooperate were Welsh (no racial bias by me intended, of course). One member of staff (also from the maths department), was forced to take early retirement after his general pathological state degenerated.

For some reason, which I have never understood, I gained a reputation for discipline. This even went to the extent of my classes acting on occasion as a "sin-bin" where naughty boys from other classes were sent. (Perhaps this may have been partly due to my techniques of class control previously mentioned.) I also had the same power as the Welsh maths head of department, who on blowing his whistle at the end of break time, reduced hundreds of milling boys to absolute silence and stillness. Oh, the sweetness of power!

I should hate to be teaching today, when the establishing of a firm routine of order is discouraged from the very earliest years. My first class in the new school was clearly the cream of the local primary schools. They were delightful and represent the joy I had, at times, in teaching. I taught them English as well, and was blessed with a group of boys who had real insight and skill in the use of English. This showed in their weekly essays. Later we were willy-nilly forced into the routine of preparing them to take the GCSE equivalent of those days. About a third of the class passed in English language, with a few less in English literature. My mathematics colleague congratulated me on my English results. His were comparable. My main subject was religious education. Here I could see little point in following a stilted and academic syllabus. I, therefore, evolved my own scheme which was apparently not objectionable to either of the head teachers. This may have been due to the fact that we were only allowed one 35-minute lesson for each class each week, not enough time to allow any written work. My scheme only applied to the first three years. There were no other RE teachers. In the first year I concentrated on the Bible, trying to explain how it is a mixture of all necessary spiritual truth about God and people, history, poetry, special pleading and plain error. The second year focussed on "God's Plan", the purpose of God as it becomes clearer through the Bible. In the third year we took the life of a human being from conception to burial, or cremation. The fourth year was open, including many "Any Question" lessons. Pupils, even the tough eggs, seemed to find this interesting.

I think, probably, that I was sometimes put upon, though I have no idea who was responsible. We had no specialist in teaching children with very limited academic ability. I was given charge of these, even though I had no training whatsoever in this field. We managed to create a warm family unit for these children, which hopefully, has helped them throughout their lives. The other notable occasion was when we started to have GCSE exams for everyone, the more intellectually gifted and those without any academic ability. Staff chose their own pupils. There remained some who nobody wanted. These were delegated to me to study the official academic RE syllabus. These were boys rising to 16 with no disciplinary pressure on them. I was comforted on one occasion by a large pleasant lad outside my group. "Mr Hammond is the best teacher of the lot," he said. Such unexpected compliments were rare.

After eight years there I had a brief period of what was then called a nervous illness and my inexplicable power of discipline was never the same afterwards. I wonder whether the Christian relationship of love was beginning to break through. Thereafter, it was a matter of teaching mixed with tolerance. I grew restless for a different future.

During all this time I was heavily involved in my local church. I had charge of some wonderful young people's groups and eventually became Sunday School superintendent. As a deacon I was a regular worshipper at the morning and evening services. On top of that, I shared in the upbringing of our three boys, especially as Hilda began to teach more and more in an infants school near to us. I fear I did little beyond essential marking at school and never brought any schoolwork home. I see now that I was imperceptibly being drawn towards the Christian ministry. I completed the Ministerial Examinations, externally tutored by Congregational ministers, with regular visits to London. At that time ministers were only ordained if they worked full-time in a pastorate. Our group of churches could not provide the payment to contribute to Church Headquarters for a full-time pastorate but only a considerably smaller sum, so I had of necessity, to return to part-time teaching at my former school. There I taught for three days per week. Under a new RE head of department, I had to stick rigidly to an arid academic syllabus – very frustrating. This was only with the first and second year pupils.

I think there was, and remains, one great deficit in the syllabus. There was no provision at all for examination courses for pupils with a high degree of manual skills – plumbers, electricians, plasterers and the like. No wonder we are short of such skilled workers now.

Chapter 6

The Christian Ministry
1973 - 2000

This has been without doubt, for me, the most fruitful period of my life until the present. Our first ministry was in Chelmsford and the villages around from 1971–79. The second, and final, ministry at Dartford from 1979–2000.

At Chelmsford I was called first to the Trent Road Church. This had been started by a Missionary outreach from the two large Congregational City Churches and so it had a heartwood of experienced and committed Christians who virtually ran the organisation. Two of these splendid Christians have since died, but the third remains one of the very finest Christians I have ever known. Worship was in the evening. There were three village churches out in the country with a very tenuous hold on the Congregational organisation. I thought they needed extra pastoral care and after preaching in them and being accepted by them, I sought District permission to add them to my pastorate. This was granted, with some misgiving. I loved leading their worship and visiting the members pastorally. Two of the churches were fundamentalist and I tried not to offend them in any way. They knew my more critical understanding of the Bible but loved me just the same. I think they had started in the evangelical revival of the 19th century and had been virtually independent. There are too many of these delightful Christians to mention individually. The third country church was in a parlous material state. The church building was huge and virtually rotting and several of the houses in this picture-book village were "owned by the church", together with an unused primary school. We decided eventually to sell the church and one of the larger houses to a local pig farmer. At that time the national church had a property adviser, a city gentleman who drove a Rolls Royce, and who did not inspire trust in me. Our District Secretary approached this adviser and I understand they made a scheme to sell all our property in the village very cheaply. One of our members was a farmer, a man of considerable determination, and there was another lady who was experienced in making executive decisions. The church community at its church meeting refused to have truck with this scheme and would only sell the old church building and one house. We converted the unused school to a place of worship.

In United Reformed Churches, the church meeting is supreme. No minister or even moderator can force it to do anything against its will, however well intentioned they are. This is not infrequently forgotten. Methodism operates in a different way, initiated by John Wesley, who was autocratic in his organisational ethos. These Chelmsford churches were organised in a group scheme reminiscent of the Methodist Circuit but operated by mutual consent and not by the authority and the plan of the Methodist superintendent minister. I spent a good deal of time pastoral visiting, as I believe this is the best way to meld a church community and enable their minister to serve them. For preaching I quickly evolved a pattern that I believe is the most effective for God's Kingdom and the reign of Jesus Christ.

This is to take a common human experience, like anger, love, shopping or leisure and to look together at what the Bible says about these conditions and activities. Then meld the two to find God's will for us now. Later the fifth church, on a long established council estate and started by outreach from one of the large Chelmsford town churches, fell vacant, as their minister had moved. I found there the ancient but always modern Christian virtues of commitment, sincerity, love and fellowship as in the other four churches. It was a busy, happy time indeed, but after eight years I felt it was time to move on. Hilda's father was widowed and we felt it was appropriate to move nearer to him.

The pastorate of Dartford became vacant. After some indecision on the part of one of the three churches I was called to the pastorate and accepted it. The method adopted by this church, formerly Presbyterian, with a strong fundamentalist element among its leadership, was to sit me among the assembled congregation after evening service and fire every kind of question at me, exploring my views on every kind of church practice and opinion. Some of the former traditional Presbyterians were appalled at this but I enjoyed it!

The other two churches were former Congregational churches that had been associated together for a long time previously. I took to them at once. One was tottering, a very small and loving congregation presided over, almost regally, by a delightful lady who was physically handicapped by illness. She had been headmistress of a local school. The sole man in the congregation had been one of her Sunday School pupils and was our excellent organist. He was like a son to this gracious lady.

The other former Congregational church was larger and very soundly led. It was in numerical decline and had severe building problems. It had sent first-class members out to many other churches. I loved these folk and I believe this was reciprocated.

To return to the former Presbyterian church, which had continued some of its Presbyterian practices into being a United Reformed Church. They worshipped in a beautiful traditional stone building, which was relatively new, and the interior was in light oak. There was, however, an element, particularly among the leadership, who seemed to be uncomfortable with me. I believe the root of the matter was that when I preached, in all honesty, I had to consider the Bible in terms of what I believe its message is to us, namely that account must be taken both of wise and moderate Biblical criticism and also, perhaps, of compelling scientific theory, notably evolution. Both, I believe, shed necessary light on the nature of God and his dealings with us. I think some considered that I should leave their ministry. You can imagine the distress this caused me as, presumably, I distressed them. Now, however, I trust all is forgiven and we are reconciled.

On learning that I would, with proper safeguards, re-marry those who had been divorced, I received a positive flood of applications to be re-married in this beautiful church building. It was ideal also for splendid wedding photographs! I married 200 couples over the 11 years I was there. I note that I had no volunteers to visit pastorally those whom I had re-married. In view of this situation at St Andrews, I retired with some sadness in 1990. The other two churches in this group have closed but in God's mercy, the fellowship of the larger has been maintained, though the members now attend other churches. We have occasional meals together.

Perhaps this is the place to express my views concerning the Christian fundamentalist position. At its extreme I understand this to be that the words of the whole Bible are accepted as literally true, or to put it succinctly, that the authority of the whole Bible is equal to that of the Trinity and is worshipped as such. This is no academic matter. Thus those not subscribing to this belief can be held not to be Christian. It appears to be widely the case in the United States and increasingly, in some measure, among British churches, including, of course, our United Reformed churches. I am aware that this position obtained generally in the whole church, until the advent of Biblical criticism in the 19th century and of popular science a little later, perhaps.

I cannot go this way for a number of reasons. Firstly, that it can lead to the grave error of interpreting the New Testament in the light of the Old Testament instead of *vice versa*. This would lead to a misunderstanding of the nature of God's love and mercy as they are revealed to us in Jesus Christ. God might then be believed in and followed as a God capable of vengeance and summary justice, instead of being primarily a God whose nature is suffering love and service, who delegates enormous responsibility and freedom to his creation in the undying hope that it, and primarily humanity, will respond to his offer of real life through Jesus Christ. This is a God who never compels but always invites, offering (at the same time), his leading and guiding, and constant help if we will accept them.

Secondly, this fundamentalist attitude must have turned many away from God in Christ, particularly those with a sensible understanding of scientific discovery and the proper methods of Biblical criticism. God is Truth and these discoveries and understandings are the gift and fruit of the Holy Spirit of Truth. Only God knows how many have been lost to faith in this way.

As Sheila Maxey, former moderator of our United Reformed Church has said, "We are not the People of the Book but we are the People of the Spirit."

Thirdly, I believe that the Spirit has led us to appreciate the wonders and structures of the universe because these demonstrate how God works with us and also to enlighten the minds of those who can tell us the origins of the words of the Bible. Therefore, I do believe that extreme Christian fundamentalists bear a terrifying responsibility in these matters. I can think of two dire warnings by Jesus that could be apposite to this situation.

Chapter 7

Holidays and My Absorbing Interests

Holidays

I suppose holidays stand out in the mind because they are unusual events, happenings that are different from the usual routine of life. Presumably they are less noticeable these days when folk are off to the continent every five minutes. In my childhood, holidays were two or three weeks in the year, and that was that.

I think the most notable holiday for me in my childhood, the early 30s, was when we went for three successive years to a place called Blue Anchor. Blue Anchor was just a row of huts along the beach by a railway halt of the same name. One hired a hut for the holiday very cheaply, I imagine, in those money straightened days. I expect the most expensive part of the rail fare was from Paddington in London. We were hauled to the West Country by one of the Great Western engines, possibly of the outstanding "King" class. Great Western engines were different from those on any other railway because of the great brass domes on top of their boiler housing.

We had to change from the main line to the Blue Anchor branch line at Taunton and I remember seeing the huge expresses rushing through Taunton station at full speed, the engines snaking from side to side. This picture has stayed with me all my life. (Always, on the journey down, we had Beauty of Bath apples, an apple now out of commercial production. They had a unique taste. I would like to get me teeth into one now!) The branch line lay directly at the back of the huts and I remember the Great Western tank engines rumbling past towards their destination, presumably Minehead. There was, I think, water laid on but nothing else. The beach was large pebbles, and beyond, an area of black mud with the occasional tree stump sticking out. This was, I think, the decayed remnant of a forest. I enjoyed wallowing about in this mud. I had impetigo there, no anti-biotics in those days. The scabs had to be scrubbed off each night. I still have the scars on my knee after more than 70 years. I remember once we had a thunderstorm, which rained very large hailstones. We packed them round our clotted cream to keep it fresh, as there were no refrigerators. We picked and ate fresh watercress from nearby. Oh the germs!

In 1949 (the year after Hilda and I were married), we holidayed with Hilda's sister, Margaret, Margaret's friend, Elma, a Scottish lass, and Hilda's parents. The holiday was in Teignmouth, Devon. I remember the ripe peaches fruiting from the bright red earth. We lodged at a boarding house owned by Mr and Mrs Barton. Mrs Barton was a somewhat eccentric lady. Men and women were allocated different cereals at breakfast. Men always had to have All Bran, for reasons of internal movement. I fear some furtive swapping went on, as I have never had constipation in my life.

This, of course, was still in the straightened times after the war. Fishermen used to go out into the estuary of River Teign and string a net between two boats, say a 100 yards apart. Then they hauled in the net as they manoeuvred the two boats together. They possibly caught two or three salmon swimming up the river to spawn. They then sold the salmon for, say, £5 a fish and must have lived comfortably on the proceeds.

Some memories concern our children. We had just arrived at a rented holiday home when we noticed that Philip, then about two, had disappeared. Frantically we searched but could not find him. Eventually he appeared from the next door's garage drive, bright as a button, crawling along the ground. Our youngest son, Martin, then about the same age as Philip, has also given us cause for alarm. One day we were lying on a beach, while Martin was paddling. Suddenly a wave caught him and was rolling him out to sea. I don't think I have ever moved so fast in all my life, as I did during the rescue.

When Martin was 14 we had a holiday in the Republic of Ireland using our Volkswagen Combi, a van which had eating and sleeping equipment. Travelling a 100 miles a day, very tiring for the driver, we traversed western Ireland. We went early on to Cashel of the Kings, a singular place with several tall narrow towers. Martin was so astonished to buy an excellent ice-cream for a penny (1d), that he went straight away and bought another. In one of the bays we saw a huge basking shark resting in shore. I believe when we stayed overnight we were perhaps unduly entertained by an excellent Irish band, nothing like the tuneless, blaring, of similar British bands. Ireland was then still a relatively poor country with excellent roads built by the Americans during the war, a sort of motorists' heaven. Time and again we saw the proverbial donkey grazing in the fields beyond the hedges of wild fuchsia. We ended up near the Burren in Galway, an extraordinary area of limestone slabs with plants growing in the steep crevices.

Later holidays, when all our children were grown up, were in Thailand and Sri Lanka. Sri Lanka was wonderful then. Our bungalows were on the beach. Every morning we saw the shrimping boats go out. I include a verse about the moving sight of these boats leaving in the morning, homing at night:

The Prawn Fishers of Sri Lanka, 2001

A hundred of them stretch against the breeze,
like rafts of wreckage, spinnakers aloft,
slow drifting, by soft zephyrs gently waft,
sail parallelograms like upright leaves.

Close to, you marvel that they put to sea
with needle hulls, outriggers lumps of tree;
a mast that leans and just a steering oar;
but prawns a-plenty they can catch, and do,
with age-old skill and a courageous crew.

Are we like them in seeming ill-designed
to sail our western life with all its pressure;
drifting maybe and often close-confined
by storms of stress and heavy waves of pleasure.

I think we only dare to join the crew
because someone is steersman whom we knew
was into catching people if he could;
to give them all the treasure of his good.

They are extraordinary, not very long, and I think, 1–2 feet in diameter, with a rough timber outrigger. There is one mast with a square brown sail, like a great dead leaf. How the crew control it is beyond me. There were about 100 of them in sight, a very moving sight morning and evening.

Outside the huts on the beach are many separate tall palm trees. Between these are strung out at 40 feet or more, light ropes, two or three at about the same height. At the end of these ropes are small metal containers gradually collecting sap from incisions cut in the trunk of each tree. Each morning a man walks these lines, one for his feet, one or two for his hands, and empties each metal container into a larger one on his back. When this larger container is full enough, he lowers it to the ground to a woman working with him, who empties that into a very large portable container at ground level and then passes up the container back to him. The liquid can solidify into a solid, toffee-like solid which is sweet and can be eaten, or is fermented to make a fiery alcoholic drink – arak or toddy. At that height the movement seems perilous but the man moves with practised ease.

Also to be mentioned on this holiday was that the campus could only be approached by ferry, as it lay towards the tip of a long narrow isthmus. This, I seem to remember, was operated by a ferryman hauling in a rope to move the ferry across. This waterway was the remnant of a canal built by Dutch engineers. As an optional extra on the holiday, we had a four hour trip along the canal with its abundant and colourful bird life being visible and expounded by a resident ornithologist. It was fascinating.

In this canal live huge lizards, somewhat akin to the famous Komodo lizards. A very large one is lured out on land by a mass of decaying meat (I presume) possibly for the interest of holiday visitors. I happened to see this huge and formidable creature on one of my early and solitary walks.

Apart from Venice, which is too splendid ever to be properly described, there is Dubrovnik in Croatia. The white marble main street *is* a marvel. We visited it before the dreadful war. I understand that the marble street is now pitted with shrapnel holes and the like. We went down the street to the harbour to embark on the best sea voyage of my life. The steamer travelled gently out to one of the outer islands. There a craftsman was selling copper plates inlaid with intricate patterns in silver and copper. I bought the smaller plate. How I wish I had bought the larger! I have never been particularly interested in seeing the great wild animals of Africa. You can see them better on television! Hilda and her sister have had several notable holidays there, including visiting the Smoke that Thunders, the greatest falls in Africa. They love seeing the animals in their natural habitat and once went to the Okovango Delta, the extraordinary inland area where a great river floods into an inland area. Hilda says that the greatest sight of her life was to stand on the airstrip in complete darkness and look up at the glory of a multitude of stars.

My Absorbing Interests

These include science, writing verse, and furniture-making. My scientific interest is especially in connection with astronomy and global warming, and the relation of science to my Christian faith. In these subjects I try to absorb any reliable information that is available. The following article is my amateur analysis of global warming. It has a very depressing conclusion. It seems that it is too late to prevent it, but the effects can be mitigated if all the nations of the world are determined to do this. They do not seem willing to do so. Thank God for the longer Christian perspective.

A Layman's View of Global Warming

I have a deep concern about the effects of global warming on the human race and on the environment, both in the present but principally in the future. Compared with the age of humanity, let alone the duration of one human life, these matters are concerned with the passing of millennia.

I have no formal education in these matters, but have a keen interest in science, notably in astronomy and in changes in the environment. My opinions are developed from thinking based on articles in one scientific magazine, in articles of reports of scientific conferences, in reputable newspapers and wherever I find balanced information with a truly scientific basis.

Our sons are trained scientists with a long experience in different fields, though not in those which interest me particularly. I have discussed these matters with them and have taken particular notice of their opinions. They all have PhDs and have doubtless discussed these environmental matters with associates who are experts in this discipline.

There is no doubt, whatsoever, of the fact of unusual global warming. The signs are everywhere. Alternate global cooling and global warming have been a feature of our planet for at least one million years and probably much longer. This is caused by the oscillation of the earth as it circles the sun. The cooling is caused, particularly in the northern hemisphere, when the earth's wobble is away from the sun. This causes ice-ages.

The ice largely melts and a warmer period ensues when the wobble is reversed. These changes follow three different defined rhythms and last over many thousands of years. These changes are therefore predictable, presumably by mathematical calculation.

A new and important factor is that, whereas our planet ought to be cooling down, according to the above processes, it is not, but instead is heating up, thus breaking the natural process. The signs of the earth's climate warming are clear to any observation.

The Arctic sea ice diminishes every winter, promising a clear North West Passage. The glaciers and the frozen sea extensions around the Antarctic land mass gets steadily less every year in the southern summer. Mount Kilimanjaro, the highest mountain in Africa and close to the Equator, has less snow around its summit than for hundreds of years. The effect of the warming in Great Britain appears, at least in the garden, to be advantageous. I do not remember all our sweet peas and runner beans flourishing, unprotected, outside at the end of April, let alone our tomato plants growing similarly with very little protection.

The possible effects of global warming in many other parts of the world are not so welcome. The hurricanes in the West Indies and the southern states of the USA are noticeably stronger than usual. The monsoons in east Asia, and particularly India, seem to fail more frequently. El Nino (the child) is a variable climatic condition occurring off the western coast of the Americas, which reverses local climates and causes flooding, and off Chile, the temporary disappearance of the anchovy shoals. Droughts are exacerbated in sub-Saharan Africa.

Much of the understanding and prediction of global warming now seems to depend on the remarkable ice-bores made in the Antarctic, Greenland and Andean areas of solid ice which can be a few miles deep on top of their land masses.

A recent such series of ice-bores made in the Antarctic penetrated between two and three kilometers. Such ice is a compacted mass of all the snows that have fallen on the area over the last 900,000 years. Contained in it are ancient pockets of air. By measuring the CO_2 in such airs, scientists can estimate, quite accurately, the atmosphere's heat at that time. The heat of the atmosphere and CO_2 are intimately connected.

CO_2 with methane and other gases are continually released into the atmosphere by heavy manufacturing industry, the burning of coal and oil for electricity generation and the heating of homes, the exhausts of countless motor vehicles, the burning of forests, the digestive systems of the world's ruminants. These all pour CO_2 into the atmosphere, thus cumulatively heating it up. This is popularly called the "Greenhouse Effect". CO_2 especially has the effect of allowing the sun's heat to raise the earth's temperature but of not allowing it to escape again, just as the glass in a greenhouse lets in the sun's heat and retains it in the greenhouse.

The great question is: Is this cumulative raising of the earth's atmosphere a natural phenomenon under all these circumstances or otherwise? Could it have been caused by combustion of coal and oil over the last 200 years? The heat of the earth's atmosphere has risen with an unnatural sharpness over this time. I am satisfied, inexpert though I am, that given all the evidence, the answer is "Yes".

This could have dire results for the future of our human race. The melting ice of the Arctic, Antarctic, Greenland, Andes and many other smaller ice-caps would be progressive under an increasing "Greenhouse Effect". This would be fresh water: I understand that about one third of the earth's water is locked up in this way.

The oceans would thus rise substantially, progressively flooding the lowland concentrations of human population. Bangladesh, for example, would be disastrously overrun. Forty percent of scientists (the figure I have read), believe that the Gulf Stream would be halted, short of the United Kingdom and north east America, by the warm northern flowing Gulf Stream being halted to the south of these areas by the icy northern fresh water flowing south. This would result in the United Kingdom, parts of Europe and north east America being reduced to an Alaskan type climate. The pampered western nations would thus experience some of the misery endured by much of Africa, South America and large areas of eastern Asia at present.

What should be the course of action for those in all this and those concerned about it? A candid view could be the cause of despair.

No power on earth, national or international, is able to deflect the increase in global warming. Nothing will prevent China's increasing use of coal for her industries, and even more for power. Her pursuit of more coal is almost frenetic. She has little oil. In the same way India, probably equally dependent on coal, is increasing industrialisation at a phenomenal rate. She too has little oil. The same applies to Brazil and some eastern countries. Again, no-one will prevent the guzzling of oil by the cars and lorries of the United States. She is also vitally dependent on her motor vehicles because of the vast distances needing to be travelled. She alone is said to be responsible for 21% of the atmosphere's pollution through emissions of CO_2, methane and other gases. And who will ever prevent the developing nations striving to attain even a pale shadow of the prosperity of the western world, and that will involve their industrialisation.

Neither is the harnessing of wind power, tide power, or atomic power from the sun's light through solar panels, going to make much difference. The fact appears to be that the very considerable cost of any of these methods far outweighs their benefit in saving the use of electricity generated by oil, coal, and apparently to a less extent, gas.

A personal example illustrates this. Recently we have had solar panels excellently fitted to our cottage roof. The whole mechanism, including the cost of plumbing and electrical work fitted independently, came to well over the cost of a new, medium value, small car. While we, delightedly, get free hot baths when the sun's disk is visible, this is, obviously, only for part of the year. All in all we do not think we are saving any electricity, as we often need to supplement by using the immersion heater. Our hot water was formerly provided entirely by a multi-point gas boiler and I believe gas is cheaper than electricity. Only my wife and I live in our cottage and we might save if more lived there.

Another example I have seen quoted in a high quality newspaper. The much disputed wind farm in the Lake District will apparently provide power for 47,000 people. A single jet airliner, travelling daily between Heathrow and New York, will make more than three times the pollution in a year than the wind farm will save. No, I believe that all that can be done to meet the dire hazard that is coming, is to use all the world's resources to mitigate the effects of the inevitable global warming. Thus all mankind could share in the easing of the unbelievable and appalling misery that is surely coming. The only course to give this purpose any reality at all, is to ensure that the stated aim and action of all governments, national and international, and every other worthwhile organisation, must be devoted to giving all possible equal benefit to every single member of the human race. Anything less than this is not a genuine sharing and nothing will cause more mockery. All else that follows will bring this into focus. I have only the faintest hope that many will take any notice of this principle, though some may follow some of the preceding and following suggestions from a sectional interest perspective.

Everything said previously, in this article, in no way criticises the measures being taken to reduce pollution. They will not stop the onset of global warming, but they may ease the present and future ills of our human race.

The ozone layer protects humanity from the ultra violet layer damaging human skin and causing skin cancer. Protection measures are relatively cheap and widely accepted by governments. The chlorine type sprays formerly used widely, could be restricted even more. The ravage caused by the escape of chemicals from factories, which have inadequate safety measures, could be even more limited. All cars could be fitted with catalytic exhausts and their fuel consumption limited. Rail, water and bus transport could be widely extended to save the real need for millions of lorries and cars.

Atomic power stations, though vastly expensive, are healthier than those using coal or oil. The world's very rapid population expansion could be limited by contraception. The constructive possibilities are virtually endless. But, taxes would be heavier and profits would be less. Even measures to promote and provide clean water would ease wretchedness for so many.

What follows is an expression of my Christian faith and its bearing on these matters. I am convinced that there will be no Divine direct intervention to save our race, but there will always be Divine support, strength, forgiveness and courage for those who choose to be open to them.

I believe the Creator created and sustains by the gift of evolution, animate and inanimate, operating in absolute freedom. Tragically, in my understanding, humanity, the peak of evolution, chose, by the freewill and choice given to it, to go the way of inverted aggrandisement and godship. This is well illustrated by the ancient Biblical myth of "the Fall".

The immense benefits of industrialisation and science have been squandered by the resolve to dominate others and to reserve privileges. There could be no more apt illustration of this than the frenetic race to build the highest skyscraper in the world. Towers of Babel, as another Biblical myth indicates.

All in all, I am convinced that increasing and devastating Global Warming is inevitably with us and that the coming centuries will, therefore, wreak progressive destruction upon our race. Much of it, it seems to me, is our own fault. However, readers will appreciate that this is not the final perspective for Christian faith.

Verse

This started in 1979 when we were in an aircraft on our way to the west coast of America to see two of our sons who were then in America. It was about a 12-hour journey. I wrote my first verses while away at the time. In the intervening 31 years verse has come intermittently, sometimes as a single poem and occasionally in a clutch. At times, the whole poem comes in its entirety; from time to time it has to be worked on to fit. On occasions, when the "muse" is present at night, I cannot rest in peace until it has been written down. It is all very odd. Of late, the verse has mostly a religious theme.

Furniture-making & D.I.Y.

This can involve the conversion of other furniture, as in the case of the two bedside cabinets I have made, or more often, the assembling of wood directly to make a small coffee table.

I have never bought any wood, just used what oak or mahogany that can be obtained from old disused furniture. The one exception to this is when I bought some wood when I was working in the mines to form the bottom structure of our former dining table. My first coffee table was made when I was 14 and of course, still at school. All the five or six that I have made since have been to the same general pattern. I remember that I gave the first table to my mother for her birthday, having requested from her the half-crown that the wood cost. I said to her "Please accept the loving workmanship!" My woodwork master at school gave us advice that I have never forgotten. "Chisels prefer flesh to wood," he said. "It is easier to cut." Since that time I have always handled tools, or knives, with extreme care. Once two mahogany bedsteads became available and these provided the wood for a small chest. I have had to stop woodworking in recent years.

I also have done all the domestic decorating until recently. This has included interior and exterior painting and wallpaper hanging. In addition, when we lived in a four-bedroomed house in Gidea Park, Romford, while I was still teaching, I re-glazed the 80 windows in the house.

I still enjoy doing the odd practical jobs in our home and garden, but I miss the creativity of making small furniture. My father had no practical skills so I think I must have inherited this capability from my two grandfathers. It ought, perhaps, to be noted that I have no skill in mechanical or electrical matters.

Chapter 8

The Blessed Present

My Christian faith has found its home in the unique Christian community to which I belong, my church. I believe that this community reflects God's will in a way that I have not encountered elsewhere in a wide variety of Christian churches and communities. It becomes my prime purpose in life to try to pass on this vision to all who will listen.

For illustration, our community to me is like the Christmas star, pointing to where the Christ child lies. I believe that, at this time, it must not be obscured by merging with any other Christian community for this may dim the star, or lose it in the mass of stars above. It must, at present, "let its light so shine among men". When its time of necessary brightness has passed, like the Christmas star, then schemes for the future will need to be considered.

Everyone is accepted in our community, whatever the nature of their Christian faith. There is Christian love of a heavenly quality. This in itself is our prime witness and mission. God reigns here.

Of course, this is not to criticise other churches or to adopt a position of any superiority whatsoever. I include at the end of this book, verses which express my understanding of our Christian faith in thought, experience, and action. The following is printed by kind permission of Rev. Lesley Charlton, minister of Kingston United Reformed Church:

"'The life of the church is all about relationships. It is not about programmes and policies; it is not in the preaching or in the organisation. It is definitely not in the ordering of the building. It is in the way that people relate. The way they relate to God, to one another and to ourselves. That is where love is found and where the Kingdom is built.

"'Firstly, relationship with God is something that requires time and effort. It is not a one-off event that happened X years ago. Taking time to be with God is what we call prayer and worship. We are not only a group of people on the earth relating well to each other, but also people whose lives are modelled on Jesus and his ability to relate. We are not a group of friends, nor a group of similar people. A church is not a club for religious people. We are people trying to know more of God and develop in our love of God. Then, having encountered God, to serve God every day.

"'Secondly, we build the church by relating to people. There was a time when people believed first and joined later. In our time we are aware that people need relationships and through them they may grow in the Faith. You may think that you are not a 'people' person; maybe you are shy and tongue-tied with others. Does this teaching mean you cannot be used by God? Not so. God does not only use the slick talkers. The words of those who pause and struggle to say the right thing are sometimes a lot more precious than the slick presentation of the easy talker. People want genuine relationships, not something that pretends to be it.

"'Lastly, what about our relationship with ourselves? Some would question that. However, let me pose the question: What is the witness of your life to someone looking at you? What about the way you rest, relax and cherish yourself? What about your ability to know yourself and learn from your past mistakes? God is known in relationships, which means we learn more of God when we listen to others'".

Lesley Charlton

1 Peter Chapter 3:15 – A Prepared Sermon

"Always be ready to make your defence to anyone who demands from you an account of the faith that is in you."

Sounds daunting to us maybe? Of course everyone will respond to this suggestion in their own way. Perhaps how I should answer it may be of some interest and may be of some help.

I think it is important to avoid using too much religious language. Most people just do not understand it. I should start by saying that I have received a challenge from beyond myself. The word "challenge" can be expressed in other words, such as an offer, promise, call, word, etc. Something has made me respond to this challenge, this word. It may be that it is due to my parents having responded. It could be from my time in the church fellowship or one or two people there, a preacher or the Bible; perhaps all of them. The response is not mainly made from Christian teaching. It is caught, not taught.

You cannot expect any outside proof of this promise in the scientific sense. It cannot be measured. It is a matter of being willing to trust that it is genuine; what Christians call faith. The only way to confirm that it is true is to confirm it within your own personal experience, together with the experience of Christians throughout the ages.

> Q. What is this offer, promise, word or challenge?

> A. It is a call from God, the being who created and sustains all things.

> Q. What do we believe this God is like? How has he acted and how does he continue in his creation?

> A. He is not a personal being in our kind of way, except when he came personally to us in Jesus Christ, but we can know him personally through Jesus Christ. He is an infinite personality.

Above all, God is absolute love in the sense that sacrificial and suffering care for all humans is at the heart of his being. He has given his universe absolute freedom to grow and develop in its own way. He does not interfere. This is the price of human freedom. Yet he is always present in everyone and everything, in love to support, encourage, comfort, lead and strengthen. He is ceaselessly present to help if we ask him. Well nigh incredible though it may seem, He is our Almighty Servant. If we respond to his call, challenge, and go his way, he offers us life with himself that nothing, even death, can destroy. He yearns for our response. If we sincerely turn to him like this he will always forgive our lack of love towards him and each other, and receive us back to life with him again. If we continue to live with him like this he gives us the power to grow more and more like him as he was in Jesus Christ.

This challenge, call, has not come out of the blue. It

came first to the Jewish people about 3,000 years ago. The Old Testament part of the Bible is the record of this, although I believe it is blurred by the prejudice and misunderstandings recorded and enhanced by the writers. They gradually became sure that God would provide the gift, to help them respond, and that this would come through a special human being. The Messiah. This happened in Jesus Christ who was the Messiah. In him God came to us personally. So the challenge and the power to respond to him is "through Jesus Christ".

In the life, death and resurrection of Jesus, God laid himself on the line for us. He showed himself as our Servant. This is what his love is like. Our forgiveness and restoration are at immeasurable cost to him. We see it in Jesus and it always has been, and will be so. Only Jesus, the man, made the proper response to God. Through Jesus Christ, we can begin to do the same. Judgement is when we turn our backs on all this.

I have accepted this offer, this promise, this call and found it absolutely true. It is the most wonderful thing in life. The crucifixion of Jesus is not God's last word in Jesus' life on earth. The resurrection is. Anyone can find the same as I have, but it must first be taken as true. It must be accepted. The personal experiment must be made. The relationship must be ventured upon.

Ps. *The events of the first Easter.*

I know that some have found the idea of the fulfilment of Christian faith as being dependent upon the one sacrifice of Jesus Christ on the cross as abhorrent. "Once for all", or "Everything depends on what he did for us then", could be said to be the concepts to which they object. I believe that this great concept, on its own, is not sufficient to express the reality of being the means to eternal life.

What is my faith is not easy to express in words, but this is my attempt. The events of the first Easter are the necessary embodiment and expression of God in human history, of what is true about God eternally. There is always a cross in the heart of God. Jesus Christ is the embodiment, in time, of what is true about God eternally. If we turn to God sincerely, he is always willing to forgive and accept us, repeatedly, in spite of what we are and continue to be. This causes him infinite and continuing agony. It is this which is embodied and expressed in the first Easter. How else could humanity know it except by its embodiment?

This mystery of vicarious suffering is one of the major themes of the Bible. This is perhaps best expressed in the so-called Servant songs in the Book of Isaiah, Chapter 42 verses 1–4, Chapter 49 verses 1–6, Chapter 52 verse 13, and on to Chapter 53 verse 12.

How can anyone have a real relationship with God if they do not know what he is like?

Chapter 9

Summing up and Onward

So I approach relatively soon, the end, on earth, of my personal journey. I hope that end may be long delayed but at 80 years old you never know! If this sounds pompous, forgive me.

I have recently had my first serious and major operation for the removal of a bowel cancer. It appears to have been entirely successful and with no evidence of cancer elsewhere. I am, thus, one of the fortunate third who have had this operation. To make matters even better, I have, literally, had no pain whatsoever. I cannot understand this but am profoundly grateful. The benefits are to be a stone lighter and a massive scar to be admired!

To commence the summing up, I cannot emphasize too strongly that this is entirely based on my Christian faith. I emphasize this great gift of faith because my living is not based on any empirical concern, fascinating to us all as these empirical matters are, but upon a faith, a trust, which is a gift from the beyond, of God. Faith is thus, a relationship.

I believe too, that without this faith there is no lasting meaning or purpose in either an individual human life or the human race. Neither is there hope or promise. As the hymn says, "O make but trial of his love; experience will decide."

If you wish to know what this experience is, look at my last poem. This is my 'awe-ful' experience and that of countless Christians throughout the ages, including those who accept evolution as God's gift and way of giving absolute freedom to humanity. A freedom too, that begins in the material, in the furnace of the stars and extends into all life as it progresses to humanity. If only the author of *The Selfish Gene* could adjust his mind to this reality. I include some of my verses at the end that illustrates these convictions. The questioning, puzzled verses alternate with those in which I trust the reality of the Christian experience shines through.

> What hope within the Crucifixion of Christ
> so widely manifest among our human race!
>
> What joy in the Resurrection
> promised and real
> for all who will turn towards God,
> now and for always!
>
> Oh happy me!
> Oh happy, happy me!
>
> Peter Hammond

So here we have the Christian experience of questions alternating with the warmth and blessing of the experience of God through Christ.

Mr. A. N. Other (Another!) Questions – A Humanist

All purpose then is nothing but a fraud;
and evolution just a wild machine
assembling out of nowhere to record
itself and crash into the dark ravine
of time? And meaning, too, is but a mould
that desiccates when brought into the sun
of our uncertainty? For when we run
to love and hope we come into the cold
bright light of scientific ways to truth?
Of course we should be kindly on our way;
(though privilege will lengthen out our days),
but nothing really matters, age or youth?
And everything is pointless; more or less
a twitch upon the face of nothingness?

Mr. A. N. Other Questions – A Christian

So I must set my trust upon a man
who briefly lived millennia ago:
and pressed into that crudely ended span
the meaning that the ages long to know?
You surely ought to tell me why I should;
why he should be the pattern for our race.
How he can be the lord of time and space?
It's not enough to tell me he was good.
You say that he will meet me on the way
I take towards him in the pressured rush
of living and enfold me in my crush
of duties and decisions every day?
Raising a heart of love into the mind
he offers unity to all mankind?

Thank Goodness!

Sometimes the empirical veil is without light
when to the thoughtful mind is seems opaque,
oblivion crouching without shape, outside.
But still the joy and warmth will filter through,
drawn inwards by the precious gift of faith;
sire blessings from the sharing heart of God
and not confined within the human mind
but spread both in and out of space and time,
offered to all who choose to share his rhyme.

My Uncle Will

Dear Will, unknown by me within his time;
killed in the Western War and in his prime;
beloved within my mother's memory file;
who treated her wild tempers with a smile.
A photograph all I have left of him
and letter to his Pa for helping him;
who lost his reason when his son was killed;
whose life, eventually, was soothed and filled.
and here am I alone in passing days
last of my family left to speak his praise.

In Christian love Will would not fight or kill;
rare in those days of war-perverted skill
A stretcher-bearer on the Front he died,
no doubt by wire and filthy mud down-tied.
Dear Will, across eternity we meet
Amongst those wondering at our Saviour's feet.

Real Freedom?

So are we trapped beneath our darkened bowls
with adamantine surfaces below,
crawling like flies, instead of living souls,
with only human means to let us know?
(the point is vital, so to make it more
we write anew and change the metaphor.)
We long for light yet cannot see a source.
The door stays shut beyond all human force,
for if with reason's wrist we try that door
we'll still be testing it for evermore.
We calculate and measure to find proof.
(No one can doubt the riches these have brought.)
From the unproveable we stand aloof
but there are limits to such human thought.

A purpose dawns beyond all calculation;
a generous offer made to us, a plan
arising first within the Jewish nation
and finding its fulfilment in a Man.
The darkened bowls have gone; the sun's in view:
with faith and hope and love we are released
into a life that is forever new,
beyond the time this universe has ceased.

The Man has joined us in our living.
We are forgiven and so forgiving.
Trimmed by the Spirit's healing knife,
we strive to live the loving life.

Perhaps a Parable?

In June I wake with dawn at half past four.
After the gulls, a sleepy blackbird sings,
surely the sweetest song among them all.
And then a tuneless twittering begins,
to drown all other territorial claims.
No doubt the sparrows contribute the most
but never having proper shape or form
except perhaps a greeting for the sun;
a repetition from the ancient past
when little birds were tiny dinosaurs
and had survived the predators of night.
And last of course at dusk the blackbird's flute
sings its finality upon the day,
blessing our faith in peaceful sleep or death
until we wake to walk the Christ-like way.

Let the gulls' cry be sad like ours as well
for all the pain and stress within our lives;
and let the blackbird song be that of Christ,
God's offer to us all of faith and hope.
So all the tuneless twittering can mean
the writhing of our race in all its life,
the disregard of all that God can give.
But last the dusk with blackbird evensong;
the proclamation that endures in all,
that Resurrection is finality
and God's eternal love beyond the pall.

The Glove

The prime reality that has been sent
is open only to faith's flickering fight
with calculation and experiment,
that obscures all but space and time and height.
So what's this miracle, unheard, unseen,
into which all things fit as hand in glove?
it is the binding on into one theme
the heavenly harmonies of lilting Love.
The wondrous all-creating Sistine hand
wound on this glove of our humanity.
No doeskin this, but a rough leather band
well tanned from evolution's enmity.
So grasp this glove, for it was ever thus
with God and all his present hidden reign.
We always live in Him and He in us;
most intimately joined, always the same.
Nothing is nearer; more closely within;
beyond all proof yet always warmly clear;
a new relationship; a second skin
transforming life, obliterating fear.
For Love never remained an atmosphere.
The broken hand bound on the mitt of flesh,
endured the rusty nail of pride and fear
and drew us out of evolution's mesh.
So praise this hand in glove with Easter joy:
in no wise cast this miracle aside.
Fight shy of means employed as death's decoy
and celebrate the Hand, the Crucified.

Where Is He?

Think of Him as an Ocean holding all;
a timeless sea where nothing is in thrall,
where all incorporate in time and space
from stars to passing thoughts enjoy His grace;
where sharks to drifting plankton have their place
and all allowed to follow after prey
as each pursues its freely-granted way.
Where fleeing fish escape the trawler's mesh
and seekers find their Home in coral reefs;
where scavengers absorb all rotting flesh
and countless fry escape pursuing teeth;
where barnacles cling to their steadfast Rock
and dolphins gambol with their family flock;
where whirling schools seek safety at their Heart,
as predators intently close and dart.
But if these thoughts seem far from Christian lore,
remember that they are but metaphor.

I'll leave You to Guess Who This Is

So fairy delicate and light
and pouring out a wonderful concern
for anyone who needs a bright
attentive hand in action or good turn
to ease the burden of some searing burn
of illness or of age's blight.
And all this with such costly caring found
for those whose temperaments are riven
by strangeness, and confusion driven
to help by rhythm or by sound.
'Love others as yourself' the Gospel says.
Remember then to love yourself as well.
O may we not allow to render mute,
the Spirit song of that celestial flute.

Sparrow Fall

We trust the Speaker, do we not,
with all that matters in this world,
concerning faith and hope and what
and where true meaning is unfurled
from out its confines in the clot
where all life's tangled twists are swirled.
So, if the sparrow does not fall outside
the Father's constant knowledge and concern,
what devastating vistas open wide
to clarify that nothing, in its turn,
escapes divine involvement at its side!

Our 'hairs are numbered', no electrons spin
in secret, all the endless spaces shared
in every rushing second, all within
the universe from start to finish, bared
to personal and suffering love, to win,
from us, response to Him who always cared.

We Seek Him Here, We Seek Him there

For those seeking to see His Kingdom way
among the varied living of each day,
it is mysterious beyond all skill.

What mind can trace the opportunity
He takes of blessing in the human will
to minister His good where He can see,
but where our probing rests on our surmise?
Or where among the dancing atoms lies
His way of mercy and of sacrifice?
And when two warring nations claim His grace
how can He give to both the Spirit's dove?
Sufficient to review all Christians' ways
and see how purposeful His footsteps tread
to lead in mercy to some greater light.

So to what ending has our musing led
and cleared our minds to understand His might?
Surely solution is of priceless wealth,
that God is in all things, without a doubt,
and all things lie within His very self.

Future

How thoughtlessly the wilful weeks rush by.
Too soon the summer vanishes again,
As always an embarrassment of fruit
blesses the table; with the thrushes mute
after their song outpouring in the rain.
So are we only watching this year die
before spring glory turns to us once more?
But listen, listen, you may hear the calling
of gentle voices, gone through death's dull door,
telling of peaceful splendours falling, falling,
upon whoever passes on to those before.
We need perspective, as we look ahead
and set our faith and hopes in metaphor:
for who can dare to measure Heaven's flow
or chart our spirits rising from the sod.
Enough to live in an eternal now,
bathed always in the love and light of God.

Real Life

I hardly dare presume to set this down:
something so precious as to be beyond
all I have written, every thought I own
which has obscured these glories through the years.

I can now understand, in my own space,
at least in partial measure, what it means
to speak of Presence and of present grace
in Christ, who shares each moment with us all:
the loving God, our brother and Life's Call.

The One who brings all hope into the now,
who sets all other things within their place,
a joy, a warmth who draws a solemn vow;
the ageless Marvel, here, within my space.